GARY POWELL

DEATH IN DISGUISE

THE AMAZING STORY OF THE CHELSEA MURDERS

D1335993

I2623220

Mum and Dad – Ron and Mary.
Thanks for everything.

First published 2014

The History Press
The Mill, Brimscombe Port
Stroud, Gloucestershire, GL5 2QG
www.thehistorypress.co.uk

British Library Cataloguing in Publication Data.
A catalogue record for this book is available from the British Library.

ISBN 978 0 7509 6025 0

Typesetting and origination by The History Press
Printed in Great Britain

CONTENTS

ACKNOWLEDGEMENTS

I would like to take this opportunity to thank several people who have given me their time, guidance and advice, which greatly contributed to the completion of this volume. Peter Kennison's unrivalled records of the history of the Metropolitan Police, its officers and police stations have allowed me to delve much deeper into the lives of some of the characters in this book. Charlotte Baker's professional editing skills were a godsend together with the photographic skills of Guy Pilkington.

I would also like to thank the staff of Kensington and Chelsea Local Archives, especially David Walker and Isabel Hernandez for their support, Amy Gregor from brightsolid Newspaper Archive Limited, and finally Cate Ludlow, my publisher, for taking a chance.

It is long since the public have been startled by news of a crime so horrible in all its features as that of which we placed a report before our readers yesterday. We need not apologise for calling attention to it in this place, because, whoever may be the guilty parties, there can be no doubt of the facts, which create an absolute certainty that two of the most horrible murders have been committed of which we have any record …

Chelsea has had the good fortune not to be associated with acts of a criminal character and the fact that it is the scene of the present tragedy is somewhat more remarkable on that account.

The Morning Advertiser, Saturday, 14 May 1870

INTRODUCTION

L ondon in 1870 was developing at an alarming rate; dozens of small towns and villages were being amalgamated to form the greatest industrial city in the world. Slums were torn down and the poor forced further east, leaving the City of London and the west ripe for development. The world's first underground railway was nearing the end of a decade of operation and continuing to expand, snaking its way across Greater London. Queen Victoria had been on the throne since 1837 and during her reign Britain led the industrial revolution and extended its reach across the civilised world.

The village of Chelsea began life during the Saxon period and gained its name from the Saxon words *Cealc* (chalky) and *Hythe* (a landing place for boats). It is situated on the north bank of the River Thames, some 3 miles from Westminster; the Thames has been an important transport artery for London over many centuries, so a location as strategic as Chelsea would always be ripe for development when the ever-growing capital spread westwards. From the Middle Ages through to the nineteenth century Chelsea was largely occupied by market gardens, but its clean air and close proximity to Westminster attracted the wealthy. Sir Thomas More (1478–1535), Lord Chancellor to King Henry VIII, moved to Chelsea in 1520 and was often visited by Henry when the king travelled to Hampton Court. Sir Christopher Wren built the Royal Hospital between 1682 and 1689. Sir Hans Sloane purchased land here in 1712, eventually becoming Lord of the Manor of Chelsea; Sloane is commemorated in the naming of several Chelsea landmarks such as Sloane Square and Sloane Street. By the early 1800s the population of Chelsea village had risen to 1,500, making it equivalent to a small town.

King's Road had a defining part to play in the development of modern-day Chelsea. It was built for the private use of Charles II to travel easily between central London, Kew and Hampton Court Palaces. Some of the local nobility were allowed to use the road – for a fee, of course. The 2-mile stretch was finally opened to the public in 1830 and this signalled the development of the more familiar Chelsea we know today. A building boom followed in the first half of the nineteenth century that saw the completion of several King's Road squares: Paultons, Oakley (renamed Carlyle), Trafalgar (renamed Chelsea), Wellington and Markham. The development of Chelsea was a great investment opportunity for any Victorian entrepreneur with spare cash.

Before 1870 violent crime in Chelsea was almost unheard of; this area was not like the dark, dank, filthy streets of Whitechapel, which would, in eighteen years' time, harbour a killer of infamous savagery. But in May 1870 the attention of Londoners and others across the country would be drawn to their newspapers as the media of the day reported, in gruesome detail, two horrific murders that shook the residents of this quiet London suburb to the core. Chelsea residents suddenly realised that no one was safe from violent crime.

The Reverend Elias Huelin, born on the predominantly French-speaking Channel Island of Jersey on 19 June 1785, was a curate at the French Protestant church in Soho and assistant chaplain at West London Cemetery (now the Brompton Cemetery). It is unclear when Huelin travelled from Jersey to England; however, shortly after his arrival he purchased a farm in Navenby, Lincolnshire. For some years he worked nearby in Sleaford and was a curate at Evedon. Huelin moved to London and the farm at Navenby was placed under the management of local resident Mr Spafford of Boothby. The earliest record of Huelin living in London can be found in the electoral registers for New Brompton which records him as a resident of No. 5 Seymour Place (now Seymour Walk), Brompton, from 1851 to 1865. The 1861 census (the first to record all occupants of the property) confirms Huelin's residence there along with his housekeeper Ann Boss. Boss originated from the Lincolnshire village of Witham South, where she had been raised by her father, a blacksmith, and her mother. The electoral register for 1865 reveals Huelin's extensive property portfolio for the first time as he evolved from a man of God to a capitalist; he is shown as leaseholder for Nos 4, 6, 8 and 9 Seymour Place. By 1867, the electoral register reported Huelin as living at No. 24 Seymour Place. It was at about this time that he started to buy larger, grander properties in the more desirable areas of Chelsea's King's Road: Paultons Square (Nos 14, 15 and 32) and Wellington Square (No. 24). By May 1870, Rev. Huelin was living permanently at No. 15 Paultons Square, a large terraced house on the square's west side, still with his long-term housekeeper. Huelin also kept a small dog, which he would often take on his rent-collecting rounds.

The premeditated and murderous events that unfolded during May 1870 have gone down as the most shameful and shocking in Chelsea's history. This book examines the events of this period using eyewitness accounts and legal records. What follows is a tale of greed, cruelty and violence which demonstrates a complete disregard for human life. The outcome is a real-life plot that has impersonation and mystery at its core; it is a story that could have come from the pen of contemporary crime writers of the day such as Arthur Conan Doyle, Robert Louis Stephenson or Wilkie Collins.

Contemporary records from the period 1870 used in this book include newspaper reports, illustrations and other sources. Some of these reports use different spellings of the names of the characters featured in this book; to maintain continuity I have used the spelling of the names recorded in official documents (death certificates, census returns and the England and Wales National Probate Calendar) that would have been supplied by the people themselves or close relatives.

G. Powell, 2014

LIST OF CHARACTERS

THE VICTIMS

Ann Boss (AB)
Elias Huelin (EH)

ASSOCIATES/EMPLOYEES OF THE VICTIMS

Eliza Bartlett, housemaid to Rebecca Evans
Charlotte Boss, sister (AB)
Robert Cox, friend (EH)
Rebecca Evans, former tenant (EH)
Edward Huelin, nephew (EH/AB)
Edward John Payne, labourer (EH)
Mrs Harriett Middleton, charwoman (EH/AB)
Miss Harriett Middleton, charwoman (EH)
Margaret Ann Millar, wife of Walter Millar

Walter Millar, plasterer (EH)
William Henry Sansom, friend (EH)
Mrs Harriett Sibley, Millar family friend
James Smith, labourer (EH)
Samuel Stainsby, tenant and next-door neighbour (EH/AB)
Thomas Humble Walker, friend (EH)
Richard Wright, solicitor (EH)

LOCAL RESIDENTS AND TRADESMEN

William Arthur, labourer
Sidney Ball, baker
Thomas Herbert, hackney carriage driver
William Pilditch, butcher and landlord
Henry Piper, carman/removal man
Frederick Vince, gas worker/labourer

METROPOLITAN POLICE

Mark Carroll, Police Constable 235T
Edward Clough, Detective Officer
Joseph Coles, Police Constable 194T
William Fisher, Detective Superintendent
Colonel Henderson, Police Commissioner
Charles James, Police Constable 273T
John Large, Police Sergeant
James Pay, Police Inspector
James Prescott, Police Inspector
Pitt Tarlton, Police Inspector
William Watts, Detective Officer

POLICE SURGEONS

Francis Godrich
Thomas Ryder
Thomas Aubrey Turner

JUDICIARY

Mr Baylis, court sheriff
Mr Beasley, prosecution counsel
William Calcraft, executioner
His Lordship Cockburn, Lord Chief Justice
Mr Collins, defence counsel
Mr Crosby, court sheriff
Dr Thomas Diplock, coroner
Mr Paterson, court sheriff
Mr Poland, prosecution counsel
Mr Selfe, chief magistrate at Westminster police court
Mr St Aubyn, defence counsel

OTHERS

Elizabeth Green, initial suspect in the murder

1

SATURDAY, 7 MAY 1870

The Reverend Elias Huelin and his housekeeper Ann Boss were, like many people, creatures of habit. Huelin was 84 years old, well-respected, plump, balding and bespectacled; he was an easily recognisable member of the district. He was frequently seen leaving his house at No. 15 Paultons Square, in the company of his small dog, to collect rent from properties he owned and let in the local area. On 24 March 1870 Huelin's nephew Edward, who had been living with his uncle, returned to the family farm in Navenby, Lincolnshire, in order to assist the farm manager Mr Spafford in securing new tenants. Elias Huelin, although a man of the Church, was a shrewd businessman with an extensive property portfolio and a sharp eye for an investable bargain. Huelin placed much trust in his young nephew and appeared to be mentoring Edward to take over his empire. Huelin visited the farm at least once a year, anxious that new tenants must be found, and Edward was expecting his uncle to arrive sometime that month.

The latest addition to Elias Huelin's property portfolio in May 1870 was in Wellington Square, a quaint garden square dotted with London plane trees further east along the King's Road. The house, No. 24, was the grandest he had acquired and it stood in the south-west corner with 'To Let' signs hanging in the windows. Reverend Huelin was a trusting, honourable man of God who was well-respected within the Chelsea community and had very few, if any, enemies. One person he trusted with the upkeep of his properties was plasterer Walter Millar, a Scot. Millar had been working on No. 24 Wellington Square for some time, often under the direct supervision of Huelin, who was keen to lease it as soon as possible. Millar was a tall, powerfully built man who, with his wife and children, had rented another of Huelin's properties at No. 27 Seymour Place since 1867, at which time Huelin and Ann Boss occupied No. 24 a few doors down. Huelin and Boss had moved to Paultons Square in 1869 while the Millars remained at Seymour Place.

This tale of violence and deceit begins on the morning of Saturday 7 May 1870, when local baker Sidney Ball of No. 200 Fulham Road delivered the weekend bread order to No. 15 Paultons Square; Huelin was one of his loyal customers. Ball spoke to housekeeper Ann Boss, who appeared to be in good spirits and who placed further orders for the following week; she made no mention to Ball about either of them leaving London. As Sidney Ball turned to leave, little did he realise that this would be the last time he would see Ann Boss alive.

That afternoon Huelin was visited by a charwoman, Mrs Harriett Middleton of Sidney Street, Fulham, whom he employed on a casual basis to clean his untenanted properties. She called at the address in order to collect her wages of 10s. She had worked at No. 24 Wellington Square under the supervision of Huelin's handyman Walter Millar, who was engaged in plastering and other odd jobs to prepare the house for letting. Middleton knew Millar from a previously shared lodging in Hope Cottage, Stewart's Grove in Fulham. Harriett Middleton, a 60-year-old married woman, was a bit of a chatterbox: she liked to talk more than work, and this caused Millar frequently to feel frustrated as he did not want to engage in conversation with her during the working day. Reverend Huelin invited Harriett Middleton into the house and gave her a glass of beer; Middleton engaged Ann Boss in conversation, deflecting her from her domestic chores, much to the annoyance of her employer. Huelin must have been satisfied with Middleton's standard of work as they discussed the possibility of further work in the future and he took down Middleton's address, claiming he would send for her when required. She left the house mid-afternoon and returned home.

John Carter was a resident of The Vale, Chelsea, and had been a close friend of Elias Huelin and Ann Boss for over twenty-five years. Huelin visited Carter's home, a five-minute walk away, on that Saturday evening. This was a frequent arrangement between the two men, who would often discuss current affairs and the property market, although it would seem that Carter had no aspirations to follow in his friend's footsteps. Carter would later recall that they may have had tea together and that as Huelin settled down to read the newspaper he realised that he had lost his glasses, so Carter lent him a spare pair of his own. The evening continued without specific mention of any intention of a trip north to Lincolnshire in the near future.

Carter next saw his friend the following morning about 8 a.m., when they both met while out for a walk in the early summer sunshine. Carter later recalled Huelin mentioning that he had been feeling unwell and would be travelling up to Navenby Farm in Lincolnshire to see his nephew Edward and intended staying for a couple of weeks. It is not clear if his housekeeper was to travel with him, but Carter knew this to be normal practice as he was aware that she had family in the area as well. Carter was slightly puzzled that his friend had not confided in him the evening before about his health or his intention to travel, but he wished his friend a safe journey and good health, and stated that he would visit him on his return. In fact, the friends were destined to meet again rather sooner than planned, and in circumstances that were to scar Mr Carter for the rest of his life.

2

MONDAY, 9 MAY 1870

P aultons Square, like many other squares in the area, had a private central garden, only accessible by resident key-holders who paid a fee towards its maintenance. Many of London's garden squares were maintained by garden committees, some introducing their own by-laws to govern the upkeep of the area. This was precisely the case with Paultons Square, which had an appointed 'square-keeper' called John Hunt, whose responsibilities included the security of the square and its inhabitants. He would have known the occupants personally, including the vulnerable and problematic, and when properties were unoccupied. He took great pride in his responsibilities and regularly patrolled the square both night and day with professional vigilance. Hunt was on patrol in the square at 7 a.m. on this Monday morning; he knew Huelin and Boss were the only occupants of No. 15 following the departure of Huelin's nephew Edward a few weeks earlier. During his patrol he saw Boss from a distance, cleaning the stairs of No. 15, but was too far away to engage her in conversation. By the time Hunt worked his way around the square back to No. 15, Boss had gone back inside. This was a significant sighting as there is no other evidence of Ann Boss being seen alive again.

Later that same morning, at 10 a.m., Hunt saw Rev. Huelin leave No. 15 and walk with a determined purpose south across the enclosure of the square in the direction of the River Thames. He returned to the square about 10.15 a.m. and continued to walk in the direction of the busy King's Road, past his own house, turning right towards Wellington Square to the east. Hunt could see that Huelin was in business mode, head down and concentrating on his forthcoming day; he was loath to interrupt his train of thought, often envious of the seemingly boundless energy the 84 year old possessed.

Elias Huelin, although approaching his 85th birthday, was a spritely, energetic man and was often seen walking between his properties at some pace. Yet on this occasion, maybe due to his previously mentioned ill-health, he elected to take a horse-drawn omnibus the half mile or so to Wellington Square. Huelin's short journey would have included sights long lost to the district, including the imposing Chelsea work-house on the corner of Arthur Street (now Dovehouse Street). This T-shaped block was built in 1843, with additional buildings (a master's house, vagrant ward and mortuary) being added in 1860. Huelin alighted from his carriage at the junction with Wellington Square. It was at this point during the short journey on foot to his property at No. 24 Wellington Square that Huelin was observed by several acquaintances.

William Sansom lived at No. 132 King's Road, Chelsea, and had known Elias Huelin for many years. Sansom witnessed Huelin alight from the omnibus, cross King's Road and enter Wellington Square, walking in the direction of No. 24 in the south-west corner. Sansom believed the time to be around 11 a.m. and noticed that, unusually, Huelin did not have his pet dog with him. He later recalled that Huelin was dressed in a new suit of clothes and was wearing a hat. No conversation took place between the two men and Sansom never saw him again.

Robert Cox, of Cheyne Walk, Chelsea, who later described himself as a private gentleman, had visited William Sansom earlier at his home in King's Road before leaving and returning to Wellington Square on other business. He confirmed the time specifically as 11 a.m. when he saw Huelin in the square. They had a short, general conversation about Huelin's health, wished each other a good day and then went their separate ways. Cox had known Huelin for some time and was aware that he was a former clergyman.

The most significant witness was Thomas Humble Walker, the occupant of No. 6 Wellington Square. Humble Walker recalled the time as 11.15 a.m. when he saw his acquaintance, Elias Huelin, climbing the stairs of No. 24 as if he were about to enter. Walker did not think this unusual as he was aware Huelin had recently acquired property in the square; he turned away to continue with his business and did not actually see Huelin enter the building.

Back in Paultons Square, the baker Sidney Ball made his usual call around 12–1 p.m. at the Huelin household. He knocked and rang the bell, but could get no answer.

The Admiral Keppel public house was located at No. 117 Fulham Road, near to the junction of Keppel Street (now Sloane Avenue), and in 1870 was a working-man's pub. Keppel Street ran almost directly between Fulham Road and King's Road adjacent to Wellington Square. Elias Huelin's plasterer and handyman Walter Millar arrived at the Admiral Keppel for a lunchtime drink about 12.30 p.m., an hour and a quarter after the final sighting of Rev. Huelin in Wellington Square. Millar arrived at the pub with purpose and had little trouble finding the man he was seeking: Edward James Payne, a general labourer who worked on a part-time basis for a building firm in Westminster Bridge Road (or for anybody else who would pay him). He was a regular at the Admiral Keppel. Payne had known Millar for about three years, often doing the odd labouring job for him.

There were no pleasantries between the two men, only an offer of work by Millar to Payne. Millar informed Payne that the owner of the house in which he was working in Wellington Square had instructed him, presumably that morning, to dig a drain for a water closet. Payne eagerly agreed to the work and Millar pointed out that he would need a pick and a shovel. The labourer drained his drink and said he would return in half an hour as he would need to borrow the tools, having none of his own. On Payne's return just after 1 p.m. he found Millar waiting at the Admiral Keppel.

Millar was relaxed, in no rush and even offered to buy Payne another drink, after which they left the Admiral Keppel around 1.30 p.m. Payne followed Millar down Keppel Street, crossing over King's Road and turning left into Wellington Square. The walk took approximately ten minutes and they arrived about 1.40 p.m. Millar took out a bunch of keys and opened the door of No. 24, and both men went directly down the stairs leading to the back yard. Millar pointed out the place where Payne needed to replace one drain with another in order to insert a water closet. Payne looked at Millar in a bemused manner and made it known that this would be a strange place to site such an item. Millar was insistent that the landlord had instructed him that it be dug where he directed. Payne proceeded with his work, thinking of his wages rather than the practicalities of the job, while Millar sat and watched

him, never leaving the labourer unsupervised. Payne dug a
hole 3ft deep and 7ft long along the base of the boundary
wall between Nos 24 and 25. Millar insisted that none of the
flagstones be moved because the old gentleman did not want
them disturbed. Payne continued with his work for just over
an hour, at which point Millar told him to stop, saying he
would need to consult Huelin before proceeding any further
and that he would work at the excavation himself.

Both men went back inside the house to the front kitchen,
and Millar told Payne to leave his tools and come back the
following morning at 6.30 a.m. to finish the drain and lay
the pipes. Before Millar left, he removed the 'House to Let'
bills positioned in the front parlour and kitchen windows.
They then left No. 24, Millar locking the door after him.
They crossed King's Road and went into Markham Street
where they parted company about 3 p.m.

Mrs Harriett Sibley, a widow of Rutland Street in
Knightsbridge, was a former lodger of the Millar family at
No. 26 Seymour Place, Brompton (now Seymour Walk),
where they occupied three rooms of the property owned by
Elias Huelin. She still kept in touch with Margaret Anne,
Walter Millar's wife, and often visited her. On Monday, 9 May
at 3.30 p.m. Sibley called on the Millars; on her arrival she
recalled that Walter was in the process of washing for dinner
and was wearing grey trousers with no shirt, just a vest. Millar
sat down to dinner in this attire whilst his wife ironed a clean
shirt, collar and cuffs for her husband. Sibley remembered that
Walter was in a particularly good mood, laughing and sharing
a joke with his company. He rather rushed his dinner and then
got fully dressed before stating that he had to go to Hornsey
in north London regarding work. He left the house at 4 p.m.;
Sibley stayed until 10 p.m. and Walter did not return.

At roughly the time Walter Millar had left his Brompton home, a tenant of Huelin's, Miss Rebecca Evans, visited Huelin's house at No. 15 Paultons Square. Miss Evans lived at No. 82 Park Walk, a short distance away. She rented No. 32 Paultons Square but had not lived there for some time; in fact she had sub-let the property and 9 May saw the expiration of the tenancy agreement. Evans wished to return the key to her landlord and had arranged an appointment for this day, but with no specific time. She knocked, rang the doorbell and waited, expecting Huelin or Boss to be at home, but for the second time that day (following the baker, Sidney Ball) no one answered. She found this strange as Huelin was a reliable and punctual landlord, especially in matters of business, and a man who loved his dog, which was currently sitting on the doorstep. She considered this odd, as she knew it was unlikely the old man would have left the small dog out, but did not think it suspicious. Miss Evans made further repeated attempts to speak to Huelin, re-visiting between late afternoon and early evening, again with no reply. Miss Eliza Bartlett, Evans's servant, also visited the house that day without seeing anyone.

Samuel Stainsby was Huelin's next-door neighbour at No. 14 Paultons Square, yet another house owned and rented by Huelin. Stainsby, an artistic actor (as recorded in the 1871 census), was on very good terms with his landlord and the housekeeper Ann Boss. He assumed that he would have been informed of any plans for them to travel to Lincolnshire to visit Huelin's nephew, with whom Stainsby was acquainted. The artist had been told nothing of the sort, but it was not until later, at about 10 p.m. on the evening of Monday, 9 May, that he was alerted to the fact that everything was not as it should be. Stainsby was a family man, married with a number of children, and it was they who told him about Huelin's dog sitting patiently on the doorstep of No. 15. Stainsby knew that if either Huelin or Boss were at home then the dog would have been inside the house, and he doubted that the elderly Huelin would be out at this late hour. Stainsby walked out into his own back garden and peered over the wall and into the back windows of No. 15. He observed that the house was in darkness, giving the impression that the place was unoccupied. Stainsby noticed that several windows were partly open and the back door was insecure, causing him concern for his landlord's safety. Stainsby, on his way to Chelsea police station to report his discovery, attempted to convince himself that Huelin and Boss had, however improbably, travelled to Lincolnshire leaving the house insecure and the dog abandoned.

Stainsby returned to Paultons Square with two police officers, PCs 235T Mark Carroll and 273T Charles James, about 11.30 p.m. (letters featured after police numbers denote the division on which they were stationed; in 1870 Chelsea was on 'T' division). After unsuccessfully attempting to gain entry through the front door, Stainsby directed the police officers through his house and into the back garden; all three climbed over the wall and into the garden of No. 15. They slipped through the unlocked back door and searched all the rooms of the house, including the coal cellar. On the first floor they were slightly puzzled by the presence of a pail half-filled with dirty water, a piece of soap and cleaning cloths lying on the floor nearby. When passing through the basement kitchen, both police officers noticed a securely fastened wooden box resting in the middle of the floor but this aroused no suspicion. They were of the mind that the occupants had travelled north, and they investigated no further. The house was secured throughout and the police officers reported their findings back to their supervisor, who instructed the local beat officer to pay visits throughout the night.

Less than a mile away at Seymour Place a handyman called William Arthur was lodging with the Millar family. Arthur was a professional acquaintance of Elias Huelin, working on some of his properties in the Chelsea area. The jobs were normally sourced through Millar, who had recently employed Arthur to decorate various rooms at No. 24 Wellington Square. Arthur had lodged with the Millars from late January 1870 and was still there on the night of Monday, 9 May.

Arthur slept on a made-up bed in the kitchen, which offered warmth rather than any degree of comfort. While Stainsby and PCs Carroll and James searched the empty Huelin residence in Paultons Square, Arthur was awoken by Walter Millar who came into the kitchen just before midnight. Arthur watched Millar prepare some supper, not dressed in his usual weekday work clothes but in new trousers and a smart grey waistcoat. Arthur broke the silence. 'You're a regular swell.' Millar, believing Arthur to be asleep, was unaware he was being observed and was slightly startled by his lodger's voice but he declined to comment, glancing at the prostrate Arthur before taking his supper upstairs. Arthur was aware that Millar had been out all evening costing future work and returned to his slumber confident of future employment.

3

TUESDAY,
10 MAY 1870

A t 12.30 a.m. on Tuesday, 10 May Mrs Harriett Middleton, who resided at No. 2 Sidney Mews, was woken by a loud banging on her front door. Mrs Middleton lived with her husband William and their daughter, also called Harriett. Annoyed and mystified as to who would wake her at such an hour, she opened her bedroom window, which faced out on to the street.

'Who is there?'

She peered down into the darkness, seeing the outline of a man standing below.

'I will answer you at your door if you would be good enough to come down,' the man replied.

Middleton was hesitant and went to the loft door to get a clearer look, where she received a similar request. Seemingly satisfied with the gentleman's appearance and tone, she went downstairs and opened the front door. She was surprised to see a well-dressed man with distinctive glasses who seemed to be of foreign origin, possibly French.

'Do you know where Paultons Square is?' he asked.

'Yes,' replied Middleton, puzzled as to why he wanted to know at this late hour. Surely he hadn't woken her to request directions?

Before she could display her displeasure, the man explained.

'I am the nephew of Mr Huelin who lives at No. 15; my uncle has gone to the country for a while with his housekeeper Ann Boss and I would like you to come and mind the place for me during his absence. I will of course pay you.'

Middleton, from the knowledge she had gleaned from Elias Huelin, knew that he had property somewhere in the country and that he had a nephew who had previously stayed with him at No. 15 Paultons Square, so all seemed to fit logically into place.

'Do you have a daughter?' the stranger asked.

'Yes I do, my eldest, Harriett,' Middleton replied, cautiously. Although she enjoyed gossiping about other people's lives, she rarely discussed her own life and family with anyone else, at least not with a casual employer such as Huelin, and she became immediately suspicious of his nephew's motives. The stranger handed over the key to No. 15 Paultons Square and asked her to report to the house later that morning with her daughter, to start cleaning as soon as possible. He stated that he would be leaving the address very early, so would not be present when she arrived. Middleton, keys in hand, was now a little more reassured that this was Elias Huelin's nephew and agreed to the request.

At 8 a.m. the same morning, Middleton and her daughter were about to leave for the twenty-minute walk to Paultons Square when they received another visitor, Walter Millar. Millar had a thick wrapper (scarf) around his neck, running from his earlobes down to the bottom of his throat, covering his face. Middleton, surprised at his appearance, enquired about the purpose of the wrapper.

'I have got a very bad sore throat,' he replied. 'Have you got the key for No. 15 Paultons Square?'

'Yes,' replied Middleton, 'a French gentleman brought it last night.'

'I want to go to No. 15 for my pails,' Millar explained.

'Me and my daughter will be there almost directly,' Middleton offered, as Millar turned to go, keeping the wrapper firmly in place with his hands.

'I'm going home for breakfast first and I'll be there as soon as you.' Millar said, as he headed back towards Seymour Place.

Meanwhile, labourer Edward Payne had returned to No. 24 Wellington Square, as instructed by Millar the previous evening, to complete the work on the drain in the rear garden. Punctuality was not Payne's strength and he arrived at 8.30 a.m. instead of the pre-arranged 6.30. Payne became frustrated as he realised that he was unable to gain entry into No. 24; Millar was not present and all his tools were inside the building. Payne noticed that the 'To Let' bills previously displayed in the upper windows and the parlour of the house, advertising its availability for rent, had been taken down.

Mrs Middleton and her daughter arrived for work at No. 15 Paultons Square at 8.45 a.m. and knocked on the door of the premises several times, unsure if Boss had travelled to Lincolnshire with Huelin. When she received no answer, she used the key to enter the property with her daughter. The square-keeper John Hunt, who was carrying out his duties as diligently as ever, was patrolling the central gardens when he saw a man whom he believed to be Walter Millar arrive at the address just after the Middletons. He couldn't be sure it was Millar due to the wrapper covering his face. The inquisitive Hunt crossed the road with the intention of speaking to him, but was thwarted by the man's quick turn of speed in entering the house, almost as if to avoid him purposely.

Mrs Middleton let Millar into the house and confirmed with him that it was empty; she noticed that he still had the wrapper around his face even when he was inside. Millar was dressed in his working clothes and noted to her that the old gentleman (Huelin) had gone to the country and that the servant (Boss) had gone with him; there was no reference to Huelin's French-speaking nephew. Millar collected his pails and left the house, presumably, Middleton thought, to return to No. 24 Wellington Square. Harriett Middleton led her daughter around the house, inspecting all of the rooms, setting out an inventory of jobs for her daughter to work through that day. She noticed the half-full pail of dirty water and cleaning items in the upper room which had been discovered by the police and Stainsby the previous night. Middleton instructed her daughter to complete the scrubbing of that particular floor first. Happy that her instructions were understood, Mrs Middleton left her daughter and returned to her own chores at home, intending to return to Paultons Square later that day.

Miss Harriett set about her work with enthusiasm after her mother's departure. She skipped down to the kitchen and saw that the fire was out, yet two saucepans were placed directly above it, both filled with cold water; one contained a partially boiled pudding. She also noticed that fresh potatoes and cabbage had been prepared in the scullery. Miss Harriett failed to pay much attention to the large luggage box situated in the middle of the kitchen floor; it was not her place to question its presence. She returned to the partially cleaned room on the first floor and would later recall with more detail what was present: a pail of water, a scrubbing brush, three cloths, soap and a flannel. It was almost if somebody had been halfway through scrubbing the floor when they were disturbed, had thrown their apron to the floor and never returned to complete the task.

Miss Harriett remained at the house all day. Several visitors called, including Huelin's close friend John Carter. Carter had had a disturbing visit earlier that morning when Huelin's next-door neighbour and tenant Samuel Stainsby came to tell him about the events of the previous night: Huelin's dog was apparently abandoned (now taken in by Stainsby's children), the house was left insecure and neither Huelin nor Boss had been seen since the previous morning. Carter visited No. 15 Paultons Square about 10.30 a.m. that morning and questioned young Harriett, whom he had never met before, about the circumstances that had led to her employment in the house. Overall she was quite unhelpful, mainly due to ignorance of the facts rather than any deceit.

Carter wandered around his friend's house in order to glean any clues as to where he may have gone or to identify anything unusual which could shed light on the situation. He went into the parlour and found an open bureau where he knew his friend kept his most private papers including the deeds to the houses he owned and probably his will and testament. Some papers appeared to be out of order, scattered on the table; this troubled Carter, for he knew Huelin to be disciplined and organised in his business affairs. Carter collected the papers and replaced them before locking the bureau and placing the key in his pocket. After repeating these actions with the alcoholic spirits cupboard, Carter searched the remainder of the house. He found nothing further of any relevance, but his suspicions were certainly aroused. The circumstances of Huelin's absence were not in character with such a methodical man. Enquiries made with Stainsby and with other known acquaintances revealed that, as far as he could tell, no arrangements had been made for the everyday maintenance of his properties while he was away. Carter thought it inconceivable that Huelin would leave for Lincolnshire without informing Stainsby or making arrangements for his properties to be managed. Carter decided to send a telegram to Huelin in Lincolnshire to confirm that all was well and, at the very least, to give himself peace of mind. Unfortunately, the telegram office was closed on his arrival and his enquiry was never sent.

Another visitor that day was Eliza Bartlett, a servant of Miss Rebecca Evans who had rented No. 32 Paultons Square from Huelin then sub-let it to a third party. Evans lived at No. 82 Park Walk, Chelsea, and had sent Eliza Bartlett to Paultons Square once more in an effort to return the key for No. 32 to Huelin, following her fruitless errand the previous day. Bartlett left the key with Miss Harriett and asked her to return it to Elias Huelin; Middleton placed the key on a peg in the hall. She had no other visitors and left the house about 8 p.m. that night.

The district of Fulham was not as affluent as its neighbour Chelsea, and the housing tended to be 'buy to let' properties attracting tenants of a lower-class background who worked in the railway and retail industries. One of these properties was owned by local butcher William Pilditch who, on that Tuesday morning at around 11.15 a.m., was hard at work in his shop situated at North End, Fulham, when he was approached by a gentleman with whom he had no previous acquaintance. The man was dressed in a light, loose suit and spoke in a variety of different accents; originally Pilditch believed the man to be Scottish, then English, before hearing a hint of Irish and French, the latter becoming more prominent as the conversation progressed.

This language barrier was soon forgotten when his visitor explained that he was interested in a particular property that Pilditch had advertised as being available for rent in Dieppe Street, North End, Fulham. Pilditch thought it strange that the man did not wish to view the property and quoted him a price of 12s 6d per week. The man stated that he wished to rent the property for a much more substantial period of time, and quoted three years. This took the butcher back a little, and he was relieved when the man said he had other business in the area and that he would return in two hours to settle a price.

The man, good to his word, returned to the shop at 12.45 p.m. and was quoted £25 per year by the butcher. They shook hands on the deal, with a quarterly payment in advance to be paid and the new tenant insisting on some household goods being delivered to the property that evening. Pilditch agreed to this request and sent an employee around to the property in order to prepare it for his new tenant's arrival. It never occurred to Pilditch to ask the man for his name or any references, presumably blinded by his excitement of letting the property to a man of such apparent good standing. Pilditch was to hand over the keys to the property when the goods had been delivered and the advance rent paid. Pilditch never saw the stranger again, and no tenant, goods or van ever arrived.

Within the next few weeks the master butcher's annoyance and frustration at the loss of earnings would turn into relief, when it became public knowledge that the foreign gentleman's luggage – should it have arrived – would most likely have contained the decomposing body of a murder victim.

Sands End was a semi-rural area of Fulham, about a mile west of Paultons Square. In 1870 it was dominated by the

Imperial Gasworks owned and operated by the Gas Light and Coke Company, the first public supplier of gas in the world; many of the local population were employed there, including a gas stoker called Frederick Vince. Vince, who lived on Stanley Road, was employed on a temporary basis commonly known in 1870 as 'odd chances'; his work was irregular and he found himself frequently struggling to make a living wage. Vince was drinking in a local pub in the Sands End area on Tuesday, 10 May at about 2 p.m. He got into a conversation with a man who had obviously already been drinking. This man was wearing a dark brown coat of some quality, light trousers and smart shoes with square toes.

'Can you fetch me a girl?' the drunken individual asked, in a French accent.

Vince replied that he 'could not, but he might get one by-and-by if he could wait'. Vince soon realised that this was an affluent man who was happy to spend his money freely and was delighted when asked, 'Do you want to earn a shilling or so?' Vince's financial position was so dire that he took any opportunity he could to earn money, and he eagerly accepted. His new-found employer suggested that they move to another public house called the Hand and Flower to discuss the task he wanted completing. Once it had been established that Vince had access to a cart, the Frenchman asked if he would be willing to move a box from one address close by to another (pointing in the direction of North End) around 8 p.m. Vince once again agreed and left the Frenchman mid-afternoon.

At some point after the discussion and offer of work, Vince must have begun to form doubts about the authenticity of the job offer, for when he met the man again at 8 p.m. he failed to bring the requested handcart. The frustrated Frenchman tried to placate him with more beer and by showing him the location of the removal job. This entailed a walk along Gunter Grove, across Stanley Bridge, along Fulham Road and into Camera Square, where they stopped for a drink in the Roebuck public house. At this point the Frenchman was nearing a state of drunkenness; he led Vince across King's Road into Paultons Square and walked to the Danvers Street end before stopping and pointing out a house occupied by a plumber and a glazier. He made no attempt to enter the premises and Vince was confused to the purpose of its identification. He was then directed back into Paultons Square to go and bring the cart to the location at which they now stood. Vince watched the man walk further into the square in the direction of King's Road and enter one of the properties on the west side of the square. Vince was fairly sober and this clarity allowed him to weigh up the odds of receiving payment for the completion of the job or being taken for a fool. He decided against collecting the handcart and simply returned home, happy that his day of drinking came with little or no personal expense.

Miss Harriett Middleton arrived home safely to Sidney Mews following her day of cleaning just as the inebriated Frenchman, under the observation of Frederick Vince, entered No. 15 Paultons Square a mile away. Finding the house empty he walked to Sidney Mews and spoke to the girl while her mother was engaged on one of the upper floors of the house. Harriett Middleton was soon made aware of the conversation between the Frenchman and her eldest daughter and that he was asking her daughter to return to the house in Paultons Square with him. Mrs Middleton went downstairs and was confronted by the man she had seen on Monday night, for whom her daughter had been working; the man who had presented himself as the nephew of Elias Huelin and had claimed he was leaving early that morning.

'You ought not to have left the house,' said the man, aggres-sively. He was dressed in the same clothes he had been wearing the last time he had made the trip to the Middleton residence, and again spoke English with a French accent.

'Then I had better go back again,' suggested the daughter. Mrs Middleton could see the inebriated state of the visitor and, concerned for the safety of her daughter in the company of this man, suggested that she return with him instead, to which he agreed. On the way he repeatedly chastised her for leaving in the first place, but she appeased him by saying how sorry she was and that she would not leave again without his say-so. When they arrived, Middleton used her key to enter and was followed in by the man who struck a light (domestic electrifica-tion had not yet reached Chelsea) and guided her downstairs to fetch a candle. He lit the candle and asked her to fetch a bottle of wine out of the kitchen cupboard, which she saw was already open, before accepting a glass of wine herself.

A short time later, at 9 p.m., there was a knock on the front door which Mrs Harriett Middleton answered. A young lady announced herself as Miss Rebecca Evans, who rented No. 32 Paultons Square, situated on the square's east side, from Elias Huelin. Miss Evans explained that she had moved out of the property some time ago and had sub-let it to a third party; the tenancy had now expired and she had come to speak to Elias Huelin to make sure that all was in order following the return of the key by her servant Eliza Bartlett and to pay the last quarter rent that she owed. She was shown into the living room and introduced by Middleton to a man who identified himself as Elias Huelin's nephew.

'I have come with reference to a key which I sent in the morning, have you sent it to No. 32?' Evans asked. The man appeared not to understand the question; Evans continued

'It was to go to No. 32'. At this stage she became slightly unnerved at the situation and decided to delve further.

'Are you authorised to transact business on behalf of Mr Huelin?'

'I am authorised to do anything for him,' he replied. Evans picked up on the French accent for the first time.

'Are you Mr Huelin's nephew?'

'Yes,' he replied.

'Is your name Huelin?'

'Yes.'

'You are not the nephew I have seen before.'

'Another, another,' he responded, waving his hand in the air with indignation. 'Have you got the rent?'

'No. I have not got it with me; I did not realise you were in or I would have brought the money, but you can have it if you come to my house.' It was quite probable that Rebecca Evans was in possession of the rent she owed, but had formed a deep suspicion that this purported member of the Huelin family was not who he claimed to be.

'I will go with you now,' the intoxicated man replied. Evans considered the state he was in and decided this would not be a good idea.

'I would rather you not,' she said, firmly.

'I will come in half an hour.' He offered Evans a glass of wine, which she declined, leaving him with the address of No. 82 Park Walk.

On Evans's departure, Harriett Middleton was instructed to follow the man upstairs with a light in order to search for the rent book appertaining to Rebecca Evans and her tenancy agreement of No. 32 Paultons Square. He led her to the bureau which had been locked earlier by Mr Carter, before producing several keys from his waistcoat and fiddling with a number of them until he managed to open it. He removed several papers and then went downstairs to leave, not informing Mrs Middleton of his destination.

Cremorne Gardens was situated close to Paultons Square and was an area of raucous entertainment with a funfair and other attractions and the location of a hackney carriage rank. Cab driver Thomas Herbert sat in his cab (number 4746) and was approached by a gentleman he would later describe as wearing a pair of large spectacles, with an imperial moustache, no whiskers, light trousers, a waistcoat and a black coat. Herbert was unaware of the sort of accent the man possessed, only understanding short passages of conversation. He asked Herbert for directions to 9 Park Walk; when advised of its location, he asked the cab driver if he could take him there. Herbert replied that he would for a shilling. The man boarded the cab and after a short distance re-directed him to No. 15 Paultons Square. Thomas Herbert watched the man approach the front door, but he did not go in, instead returning to the cab and ordering Herbert to take him to the original destination.

On arrival at No. 9 Park Walk his passenger made some enquiries with the householder, who looked at Herbert and commented that they could not understand what he was saying and asked the cab driver where he had brought him from. Herbert put the communication difficulties down to the man's inebriated state. The man returned to the cab with a drunken determination to find the location he was seeking.

'It is either No. 9, 7 or 5,' he shouted.

Next he tried No. 7, knocking loudly at the door regardless of the time of night. An irate gentleman opened a first-floor window and asked who was there. Neither the householder nor Herbert could understand the strange language being used. The householder – who could speak both French and

Italian – tried to converse with him, but he seemed unable to understand the drunken man either, which surprised Herbert, as he believed the man to be French. The now impatient householder demanded that Herbert take his passenger home. Herbert's passenger was insistent they find the person he sought and repeated the whole episode at No. 5, with the same result. Now disgruntled, he got back into the cab and asked to be taken back to No. 15 Paultons Square.

On his arrival, he was met at the front door by Harriett Middleton and asked her if she could recollect the number of the cottage he had to go to in order to receive the lady's rent. She couldn't. The man told Thomas Herbert to return him to Park Walk where he would try Nos 44 or 45 and ask around the neighbourhood, in his drunken stupor, to see if they could provide any additional information as to where the lady lived. Herbert was quite happy to oblige as the fare grew with each trip to and fro. Herbert's passenger then proceeded to knock firstly at No. 45 but got no reply, followed by No. 44, whose occupant threatened him with incarceration for disturbing him if he did not go away. Finally defeated, he was taken back to Paultons Square where he invited Herbert in for a glass of wine, which the cabbie accepted. Herbert was told to return the following night when he would be paid the sum of 10s.

4

WEDNESDAY, 11 MAY 1870

Mrs Harriett Middleton spent the night in the kitchen, exhausted, propped up against the wooden box, not daring to leave; she did not see the Frenchman until late Wednesday morning when he asked her to go and get him another bottle of wine. He drank it and gave Middleton 2s, instructing her to remunerate Thomas Herbert when he returned to the house later that night. Rebecca Evans's servant Eliza Bartlett paid a further visit to the house, sent by her mistress to find out why the man purporting to be the nephew of Elias Huelin had not collected the rent from her the previous evening. Bartlett was shown into the back parlour by Middleton, where she saw the Frenchman for the first time. She assumed this was the man her mistress had sent her to see as he appeared precisely as Evans had described: wearing a light waistcoat, a frock coat which she believed to be black, a high hat and spectacles. Bartlett questioned him about the key she had delivered to the address and handed to Miss Middleton the previous day:

'Did you deliver the key to No. 32?'

'Me have no key,' he replied in broken English, somewhat surprised. At this point Harriett Middleton retrieved the key from the hook in the hallway, where her daughter had placed it the previous day, and gave it to him.

'Me will send it to No. 32,' he offered. He handed it back to Middleton who replaced it on the hook. He continued, 'me could not find it.' Bartlett assumed from his comments that he was referring to her mistress's address the night before. He took a card from his pocket and showed Bartlett the number forty-seven written on it. She informed him that it was the wrong number and gave him the correct address of No. 82 Park Walk. The gentleman said that he would call on the house within half an hour and offered Bartlett a glass of wine, which she declined. She left the address, returning home and reporting the conversation to Rebecca Evans.

Shortly afterwards the Frenchman departed, leaving Middleton to clean the house for the rest of the day. She did not see him again until much later that night. The Frenchman arrived at No. 82 Park Walk and was met by Eliza Bartlett, who answered the door and showed him into the house. Evans recalled that he was wearing the same clothes that he had worn the night before, but minus his spectacles, and asked him if his name was Huelin, to which he replied, 'Yes.' The man pressed Evans for the outstanding rent, confirming that he was quite authorised to collect it on his uncle's behalf. Evans' suspicions grew.

'I will not pay it to you, I would rather pay it to Mr Huelin or his housekeeper.'

'My uncle will not be at home.'

'When *will* he be at home?'

'They are coming home tonight, about eleven o'clock,' he replied, hesitantly, seeming to make it up as he went along.

'We will see them tomorrow morning,' Evans replied, sensing that something was indeed amiss.

'They are going off early tomorrow morning and will not be home for a fortnight, I will call again tomorrow for the rent.'

'I would rather see Mr Huelin,' she said, relieved her visitor had now turned to walk away. The Frenchman would not return to No. 82 Park Walk and the next time she saw him would be under very different circumstances.

Following his frustrating meeting with Rebecca Evans, the Frenchman travelled to the West End for some entertainment. He chose the notorious areas of Soho and Haymarket. He had money in his pocket and spent freely in the clubs and pubs of the area. Later that afternoon, while walking along Windmill Street, he saw a young woman whom he engaged in conversation and discovered that her name was Elizabeth Green. The young lady was attempting to make some money by selling lights on the street.

'You had better put your lights in your pocket and come with me,' he said to Green. 'Will you have anything to drink?'

'Yes,' she replied, eagerly, 'I don't mind if I do, for I am cold and wet.' The Frenchman took her into a nearby public house and bought her a drink. He then escorted Green to a fashionable store and bought her a hat, jacket, skirt and a new pair of boots. For the next few hours and well into the evening, he plied Green with drink to the point that she was incapable of looking after herself. She would remember being placed in a fly (a lighter, quicker horse-drawn carriage), not a cab, and being taken to a house in Chelsea, an area of London with which she was unfamiliar.

During the journey from the West End to Chelsea, the Frenchman ordered the fly to divert and turn right into Marlborough Road (now Draycott Avenue) just off the

King's Road, near to Sloane Square. The fly stopped outside the address of the greengrocer and van proprietor Henry Piper. The time was about 9.20 p.m. and the shop was shut. The man knocked on the door and Piper answered.

'Do you have a machine or a cart?' the Frenchman asked.

Piper was unsure if he fully understood what the man was asking for, finding his accent hard to decipher.

'What do you need me to do?'

'To move some luggage.'

'When do you want it?'

'In half an hour's time.'

'What will the job come to?' asked Piper. The man failed to understand. Piper made it clearer. 'What shall you pay me if I come at this time of night? It is now pouring with rain and very late.'

Piper's visitor now seemed agitated and barked impatiently. 'Me pay you anything you charge, you make your charge and I will pay.' He put his hands into his pockets and rattled the coins therein in order to show that he was good for the money. 'I want you there in half an hour.'

'Where?' enquired Piper.

'15 Paultons Square.'

'Where is the load to go?'

'To Fulham, the West End.'

Piper agreed to be at Paultons Square at the stated time. He watched the Frenchman walk to his carriage and disappear in the direction of King's Road.

It was gone 10 p.m. when Harriett Middleton opened the door to the Frenchman (who was still wearing the same clothes) and Elizabeth Green, a woman whom she had never met previously. Middleton was asked to go and fetch another bottle of wine, which she did. The man drank most of the wine himself, offering a little to the already intoxicated Elizabeth Green. Middleton was then instructed to go to the bedroom and cord up all the bedding in order that it may be removed, with the box in the kitchen, that night. Its destination, she was told, was the old gentleman's house in the country. It was while performing this task that there was a knock on the door. She answered the door and immediately recognised the visitor: Henry Piper, a popular and respected figure in the Chelsea community. Piper had brought along another man, George, to assist with the removal. Piper explained why he was there at such a late hour and asked Mrs Middleton if there was some luggage to go away from there that night? Middleton confirmed that there was and invited him into the hall, leaving George outside to guard the cart. As Piper stepped in, he was met by the man he had seen earlier that evening.

'Where is the luggage, sir?' enquired Piper, anxious to get on with the job because of the late hour.

'Some upstairs and some down,' was the reply.

Piper made to go upstairs when the man said, 'Downstairs first, follow me.'

Piper, Green and Middleton, who had a light, followed him downstairs. Before entering the kitchen, the Frenchman put his hand into the front parlour which was facing the foot of the kitchen stairs and removed a piece of rope, which he seemed to find with little difficulty, even in the darkness. He then led Piper and Middleton into the back kitchen where the box – already seen by Samuel Stainsby, the two police constables who had searched the address two nights earlier and both the Middletons – stood under the wall on the left-hand side.

'I want the box corded,' the Frenchman directed.

'It don't require cording, it will stand in the bottom of the van,' replied Piper.

'I will have the box corded,' insisted the Frenchman, 'and I will cord it myself.' He attempted to cord the box around its middle, but Piper pointed out that this was the wrong way to do it and took the cord out of his hand, formed a loop around the end and slid it under the box. The Frenchman looked on anxiously as Piper got the cord around the lock and fully under the box. He picked up the other end of the box with his left hand and lifted it on its end to make it easier to lift. He felt something sticky and moved into the light Middleton was holding. Thick red blood coated his hand. Piper showed it to the Frenchman and demanded to know, 'What does that mean?' He didn't immediately answer and seemed genuinely surprised. Meanwhile, Piper moved the box further away from the wall and saw a pool of dark congealed blood on the floor where the box had originally been resting. Piper – now quite angry – again asked the man for an explanation for the presence of what he believed to be blood emanating from the bottom of the box. He received no reply.

'Mrs Middleton, do you know anything of this?' Piper asked.

'No, the box was there when I came in, and there it is now,' she replied, horrified. Suddenly, with one movement, the desperate Frenchman wrenched off, over his head, the light coat which he was wearing and threw it down onto the pool of blood and stamped on it. Piper was at some disadvantage as he had the box half-suspended and was resting the weight on his hip. He remonstrated with the Frenchman, saying that he would move the box no further until he showed him what was inside. Elizabeth Green, even through her drunken stupor, realised something was seriously wrong, turned clumsily and headed back up the stairs. The Frenchman picked up his now blood-soaked coat from the floor and followed. Piper placed the box back on the floor and quickly followed them both up the stairs. The Frenchman stopped halfway up, realising the removal man was in pursuit. 'Go back, and cord that box!'

'Not me,' replied Piper, now positive that something awful had occurred and determined to find out what.

'Go back, you carman,' the Frenchman retorted, stamping his feet on the stairs in an effort to intimidate Piper, 'and cord that box and do your work.'

'I shall not!' replied Piper, defiantly. 'I don't mean to lose sight of you.' Piper noticed that as the man lost his composure, he also lost his accent, which was replaced by an English one.

Piper followed him out of the front door, into Paultons Square, where he saw him turn left heading toward King's Road. He put the bloodstained coat back on as it was still raining. Piper stayed within a short distance of the man and saw a police constable, Joseph Coles 194T, standing under a lamp post at the junction of the square and King's Road. Piper went up to PC Coles and told him his name, while the Frenchman remained nearby. Piper explained to the constable the sequence of events that had brought him to No. 15 Paultons Square; the cording of the box, the discovery of the pool of blood and the behaviour of the man since that discovery. The inexperienced PC Coles seemed hesitant as to what to do and suggested that all three of them return to the house in Paultons Square and investigate the mysterious circumstances, believing there was probably a perfectly sound explanation which would resolve their conflict.

As they were about to enter the house, Piper touched PC Coles on the shoulder and advised him that should he go into the house they would lose the Frenchman. Piper, noticing the reluctance of the officer to make a decision, turned to his mate George, who had remained by the cart.

'Run, George! Up to the station and tell them to send some more men down to 15 Paultons Square. Tell them who sent you.'

George, following the instructions of his employer, immediately broke into a run in the direction of King's Road and Chelsea police station, which was located only a quarter of a mile away, adjacent to Park Walk. The Frenchman, still technically at liberty, was now getting very fidgety, walking backwards and forwards and shadowed by the ever-vigilant Henry Piper and the apprehensive PC Coles. Piper again implored PC Coles to, 'Lay hold of him, he will bolt directly.' Suddenly Piper's fears were realised as the Frenchman made a break for freedom, running towards Danvers Street at the square's southern end.

'There now,' Piper shouted, 'he's gone!' Piper and Coles chased the Frenchman, who was running at great speed; luckily Piper was a fit individual and kept pace, but PC Coles started to lose ground on the fleeing man. As the suspect ran, he discarded his hat and then pulled off his coat and threw that on to the ground. Piper shouted at the top of his voice the first thing that came to mind, 'Stop thief!' and 'Murder!' He ran along the length of Danvers Street, turning left into Lombard Street, which ran adjacent to the River Thames. Lombard Street was a narrow, commercially busy area, with several drinking establishments; a number of people were standing in the street but made no move to react to the desperate pleas of Piper to apprehend the apparent fugitive. However, the suspect, while passing the bystanders, slipped off the steep wet kerb and fell on his face. Piper was within 10 yards of him and was upon him before he could escape again. Piper had hold of him now and was not going to let him escape again, convinced that he was responsible for some terrible crime. PC Coles arrived shortly after and also restrained him.

'We will take him now,' the young officer panted, 'I don't want anything else. I know he has done something wrong or he would not have run away.'

Elizabeth Green, realising through her drunken haze the awkward position she found herself in, quickly made good her escape, walking off in a different direction to that of the prisoner and Piper. It was very doubtful that Green had any knowledge of what had taken place and she later claimed she had no idea as to why she had been brought back to the house and for what purpose. The intoxicated Green found herself in an area of London to which she was very unfamiliar, and it was in this state at about 1.15 a.m., some three hours after making a hasty exit from No. 15 Paultons Square, that she was arrested for being drunk in a public place. She was then taken to Walton Street police station in Kensington where she was kept in custody until the following morning when she appeared before magistrates and was given a conditional discharge with a warning for her behaviour in the future.

Piper and Coles walked their prisoner back to Paultons Square. On their arrival, the reinforcements had appeared in the shape of Police Sergeant John Large 1T and a couple of constables. Sergeant Large was an experienced police officer, having joined the Metropolitan Police force in 1855; he had served on the division most of his career and knew the area and its people very well. Large had listened to what had occurred and took instant control, instructing Coles and another constable to take the prisoner to Chelsea police station.

Chelsea police station, with section house accommodation, was situated on King's Road at the junction with Milman's Row and was built in 1852 at a cost of £1,500. It was a substantial three-storey brick building with a charge room and three cells, a standard design for police stations being constructed around the capital as the Metropolitan Police, founded in 1829, grew in size. The rapid pace at which Chelsea was being developed was recognised by the police hierarchy in 1855 and they noted that the police strength and its effectiveness to patrol this district needed to be urgently reviewed. A report by the Metropolitan Police identified that the district had grown by some forty-four streets and four squares since 1849, with the average length of a constable's beat increasing from 1,100 yards to 2,000 yards even though fifteen new beats had been introduced.

On arrival at the police station PC Coles searched the man in his custody. His prisoner, whose identity had not yet been established, refused to answer to any questions put to him at this early stage. The search revealed the following items: £7 10s in gold; 9s 6d in silver; 5½d in bronze; a corkscrew; two knives; a pipe; a pencil case; a pair of spectacles in a case; three gloves; a common ring; a bloodstained abstract of the title deeds to No. 24 Wellington Square, Chelsea (found in the coat discarded by the prisoner during the chase); two envelopes addressed to 'Miss Boss, 15 Paultons Square'; a rent book; a silk handkerchief; the remnants of a broken bottle evidently smashed during the fall prior to his arrest; and a bunch of keys on a ring. All this property was handed to the station officer, Inspector Pitt Tarlton. Tarlton was a no-nonsense copper from Southern Ireland who had risen up the ranks at speed but had the respect of his peers. He, unlike Sergeant Large, had served on other divisions before he moved to Chelsea on his promotion to inspector.

Meanwhile, back at No. 15 Paultons Square Police Sergeant Large, Henry Piper and Mrs Harriett Middleton returned to the back kitchen. Piper pointed out the partially corded box on the floor, precisely as he had left it only ten minutes before. He explained again what exactly had happened and the circumstances in which he found the box, pointing out where it had been positioned before he had moved it and discovered the blood on his hand and on the floor. Sergeant Large saw that the wooden box was of some age and green in colour, and he estimated the size to be 2ft 11in long, 1ft 6in wide and 1ft 7in deep. It was locked as well as partially corded. He moved the box to the side and saw a quantity of blood on the floor. Large took a poker from the nearby fireplace and broke open the lock with it. As the fastening was released, the lid of the box sprang open several inches as the compressed head and shoulders of a dead woman popped up like a macabre jack-in-the-box, a horrific expression of terror contorting her face. The cold body was of a diminutive female who had been treated with shocking barbarity, shoved doubled-up inside the box. They were hit by an aroma of death and decay; it seemed that the unfortunate victim had been there some time. Large and Piper stepped away momentarily and Mrs Middleton screamed. She looked deeply in shock. Eventually she managed to confirm, to all present, that the woman in the box was Reverend Elias Huelin's housekeeper – Ann Boss.

Sergeant Large called for a local doctor, Thomas Ryder, to attend the scene. He responded quickly and found that the body of the deceased had not been moved. He noted that she was fully dressed and a rope around her neck was fastened in a double knot. The rope was so tight that he could not get his finger between it and the victim's neck. This was determined as the cause of death as there were no other evident injuries. Ryder also noted that blood had poured from the nose and mouth of the victim, resulting from the congested condition of the brain which had caused extensive rupturing of blood vessels; this was due to the stricture around the neck not being removed. Dr Ryder estimated that maybe as much as two quarts of blood had saturated through the box; a fact the murderer, when strangling the victim, hadn't bargained for.

While Dr Ryder was examining the scene, Sergeant Large removed the rope tied around the unfortunate victim's neck. He then compared the rope on the victim's body with that of the cord used on the box and concluded that they were the same. He left the body in situ and returned to the police station where the prisoner, now suspected of the murder of Ann Boss, was being held. Large made enquiries with Inspector Tarlton about any keys being found in the possession of the prisoner and was handed the bunch that were found during the earlier search. Large returned to Paultons Square and matched a key to the lock on the box in which Boss's body had been found.

Back at Chelsea police station Inspector Tarlton's attention was drawn to the broken bottle found in the prisoner's right-hand trouser pocket. The neck of the bottle was complete with the cork still lodged in the opening.

'Why!' he exclaimed on closer examination, 'This is a poison bottle.' The prisoner, who was until this point standing, dropped down and bent over with his hands down by his side; he remained silent. The inspector asked the arresting officer, PC Coles, if the man was drunk. Coles said that was 'not possible as he had run at such a fast speed to evade his capture earlier on'. Inspector Tarlton immediately sent for another surgeon, Dr Francis Godrich, to examine the prisoner.

On Dr Godrich's arrival he was told about the circumstances of the arrest and the subsequent discovery of a bottle of poison. He was also informed that the prisoner was thought to be French. Godrich saw that the prisoner was now lying on the floor and spoke to him in both French and English, but received no response. Godrich observed that the prisoner was both pale and weak and was unable to move his limbs and was unwilling to try. The doctor was shown the remnants of the bottle and some broken shards of glass in a piece of paper. The visible label read 'Laudanum' (an opium derivative widely available in Victorian England) and was accompanied by a spicy aroma associated with the drug. Godrich, thinking the man may have taken the drug, gave the prisoner an emetic with coffee and brandy, which he drank freely. Godrich came to the conclusion that it was unlikely the prisoner had taken the drug (although it was widely reported in the press, over the next few days, that the prisoner had taken the poison in an effort to kill himself). Godrich informed Inspector Tarlton that he believed the prisoner to be 'shimming insensitivity' for his pupils acted naturally and his pulse was regular, though weak.

There was great speculation in the contemporary media that the police believed the woman who fled the house in Paultons Square (Elizabeth Green, yet to be identified) on the night the body of Ann Boss was discovered was complicit in the murder, and that she could have been a man dressed as a woman. When Green's identity was discovered and she was traced by the police, it was established through questioning and other reliable pieces of evidence that she was merely an unfortunate, naïve participant who had been in the wrong place at the wrong time.

The police now had a murder victim, a suspect whose identity was unknown and a possible motive with the finding of the deeds to No. 24 Wellington Square. Could Rev. Elias Huelin be another victim of the callous murderer they had in custody, or was it possible that the missing former clergyman could be complicit in the murder of his housekeeper, Ann Boss? The police had to find Elias Huelin as soon as they could, but where would they begin their search?

5

Thursday, 12 May 1870

The police had a suspect who refused to speak and who, according to witnesses, had purported to be the nephew of Elias Huelin of No. 15 Paultons Square, Chelsea. The man failed to confirm or deny his identity at the police station and, following the laudanum incident (whether he took the drug or not), the police were reluctant to interview a murder suspect officially as any later reliance on what he said could be deemed flawed. They were sure they had the man responsible for the murder of Ann Boss; the evidence they had (discussed in detail in a later chapter), indicated that he was the killer or at least complicit in the murder.

On the morning of Thursday, 12 May 1870 the detective branch of the Metropolitan Police was called in to take over the investigation. The Metropolitan Police force was created in 1829 and was initially an organisation focused on the prevention of public disorder and the safety of the public in general. It was not until 1842, following a substandard murder investigation in which murderer Daniel Good evaded police for a long period of time, that the detective branch was set up to investigate serious crime. The Scotland Yard detectives allocated to this murder investigation would work under the leadership of 'T' division commander Superintendent William Fisher. Fisher had taken charge of 'T' division in May 1868 and was based at Hammersmith. One of the initial tasks Fisher carried out was a team briefing: discussing and examining the evidence that they had collated already, what the witnesses were saying and the significance of the property found on the suspect. From this discussion he identified lines of enquiry that would need immediate action. Shortly after the briefing, Fisher sat down and recorded all the facts of the case on a morning report (National Archives MEPO 3/97); the record was detailed and specific, noting that Dr Ryder had estimated that Ann Boss had been dead for two or three days. Fisher instructed Police Inspector James Prescott, as a matter of urgency, to travel north to Navenby in Lincolnshire to establish if Elias Huelin had ever arrived at his farm to visit his nephew Edward. The police needed urgent confirmation that Huelin was not in fact alive and well 100 miles away. Of course, at this early stage of the investigation it could not be ruled out that the missing man's nephew, Edward Huelin, was in fact the man sitting in the cells at Chelsea police station and responsible for the murder of his uncle's housekeeper. One thing was clear in the mind of the investigating officer as he concluded his report (National Archives MEPO 3/97): 'The prisoner (identity at this stage still unknown) is at present unable to reply to any questions, but he will, when sufficiently recovered, be charged on suspicion of having committed murder.'

Detective Inspector James Pay was instructed to investigate the location of the last confirmed sighting of Huelin at No. 24 Wellington Square. Pay obtained information from Mrs Harriett Middleton that the person to speak to about this property and the possible location of Elias Huelin was his maintenance man, Walter Millar. On the morning of Thursday, 12 May Pay went to No. 26 Seymour Place to trace and interview Walter Millar. Pay knew that Millar was possibly one of the last people to have seen Huelin alive: Millar had turned up at Harriett Middleton's house on Tuesday morning asking if she had the key to No. 15 Paultons Square before visiting the house to pick up his pails a short time later. The fact that the Middletons had seen the Frenchman purporting to be the cousin of Huelin on several occasions that week, and that both Middletons had known Walter Millar over a much longer period, eliminated the plasterer as a possible suspect, so Inspector Pay was keen to interview Millar as a source of information regarding the last movements of his missing employer.

Inspector James Pay had joined the police at the age of 18 in 1851, recruited while attending the Great Exhibition in Hyde Park, and was an extremely capable investigative officer. He went to the address with a view to interviewing a potential witness, but as an experienced detective he would keep an open mind to all possibilities and follow any trail to which the evidence led him. The door was answered by Walter Millar's wife, Margaret Ann Millar. She was asked if her husband was in and informed the inspector that he would be at work. Pay sought information from Margaret about the Millar family's domestic circumstances in order to paint an accurate picture; he gleaned from her that they had two children, one of whom lived with them in London while the elder was in Scotland. Pay noticed that Margaret Millar was also pregnant. Pay was aware that from the witness evidence gathered so far it would seem that the last time Millar was home was late on Monday night when William Arthur had seen him taking a late supper. So when Mrs Millar confirmed to Inspector Pay that she had not seen her husband for at least two nights, this aroused his suspicion. Mrs Millar was asked to accompany Inspector Pay to Chelsea police station so a detailed statement could be taken.

The suspect for the murder of Ann Boss remained in custody at Chelsea police station and was deemed to be in a profound state of depression, whether due to the predicament in which he found himself or to the intake of a small dose of laudanum. The doctors were in agreement that he was in no fit state either mentally or physically to be detained at the police station any longer and arrangements were being made to transfer him – still in the custody of the police – to St George's Hospital at Hyde Park Corner (now the Lanesborough Hotel). This was a blow to Superintendent Fisher's investigation as he wanted the opportunity to sit down with this man and interview him about the growing mountain of evidence being compiled against him. Just before the prisoner was due to be transferred to hospital Inspector Pay and Mrs Millar arrived at the police station. Pay had a hunch, a gut feeling that police officers often rely on – a copper's nose, sensitive, probing for the truth. He was about to take the biggest risk of his police career so far. A deeply shocked Mrs Millar was taken into the cell complex and Pay watched her face intently as the suspect for the murder of Ann Boss was brought into the charge room from the cells. Margaret Millar at first seemed bemused, trying to understand what was going on and wondering why she had been brought into the custody area. She was confronted by a man she did not at first recognise, a man suspected of the violent premeditated murder of a 40-year-old housekeeper. She looked at the man in his fine clothes and spectacles; he was clean shaven apart from a small thin moustache and a tuft of hair on his chin below his lower lip. He looked drawn and defeated, a man who was facing death. Mrs Millar looked at Inspector Pay, desperate for all this to be some huge mistake.

'Mrs Millar, is this your husband?'

'Yes,' she replied, 'this is my husband, Walter Millar.'

Inspector Pay returned with Mrs Millar to the family's rented house and carried out a systematic search of the property. In the ground floor front room Pay searched a box in which he found an abstract of title deeds for the property at No. 2 Trafalgar Square, Chelsea (the name was changed to Chelsea Square in the late nineteenth century to avoid the obvious comparison with the square in Westminster). On the front of the deeds, written in pencil, were the words 'Elias Huelin, No. 15 Paultons Square'. Also in the box was an envelope addressed to Rev. Huelin, an estimate of some work to be done, a catalogue of ten houses and eight keys on a ring. The next piece of evidence Pay found was in the bedroom, and of extreme significance – a pair of light trousers stained with two or three faint spots of what appeared to be blood. Mrs Millar confirmed to Inspector Pay that the trousers belonged to her husband. All of the articles found were seized by the detective to form part of the prosecution case.

The next few days were extremely frustrating for the police investigation as they were unable to interview Walter Millar, now an inpatient at St George's Hospital, regarding his part in the murder of Ann Boss. The police search of No. 15 Paultons Square had revealed no other clues to establish the whereabouts of Elias Huelin; it was at this point they turned their attention to No. 24 Wellington Square.

Inspector Pay had been unable to find keys for No. 24 from the bunch found on Millar or other keys found at Millar's house, and had to gain entry by climbing No. 23's high garden wall. Pay made a cursory search of the empty property, the smell of fresh paint filling his nostrils as his footsteps echoed, bouncing off the walls of the unfurnished, empty rooms and carpetless floors. He noticed dark red smears on the floor of the kitchen, which he believed to be blood; the marks were in a circular pattern giving the impression that an attempt at cleaning had been made in a hurry. He also noticed what appeared to be bloodstains on the back of a small concealed cupboard under the stairs.

At 2 p.m. on the Thursday afternoon murder detectives Edward Clough and William Watts entered No. 24 Wellington Square and were briefed by Superintendent Fisher and Inspector Pay. Fisher was now convinced that the missing man was concealed somewhere within the building. The main focus of the initial search was the back kitchen where Inspector Pay had found the traces of blood. Clough found a pick and shovel near to the back door leading to the patio and garden. If the body had been concealed within the house, as all present now suspected, a systematic search would have to take place which would include the dismantling and removal of floorboards, fixtures and fittings.

Indications were appearing on a regular basis that Elias Huelin had been murdered and concealed somewhere in this house. The discovery of bloodstained paper in the yard was a critical find and supported the theory. Clough recalled later that the paper looked as if it had been torn from the wall and used to soak up the blood from the floor. This discovery gave the team the focus and motivation to continue in their search. No word at this stage had been received from Inspector Prescott to confirm whether Huelin had travelled to Lincolnshire or not.

Superintendent Fisher knew the probable answer and pushed his men to find the missing body. Just as the search team's efforts were ending for the day, a significant discovery was made under the floorboards between the rafters in the back kitchen near to the sink: a blood-soaked cap with a gaping hole on one side, possibly caused by a blunt instrument such as a shovel. Edward Clough was in no doubt that the cap, the lining still damp with congealed blood, had been concealed.

The pressure from the public and the media to find the missing man was growing with every hour. The police knew that Elias Huelin had probably been murdered and there were obvious signs of a violent struggle having taken place within the house, yet so far no corpse had been uncovered. The detectives were fairly sure that the body must be concealed in the house; it was unlikely that Walter Millar, if indeed he was the murderer of Huelin as well as Boss, would have had time to move the body on the day of the murder. The police were already constructing a specific timeline of his movements between Monday and Wednesday night from witness statements. The location of Elias Huelin – dead, as strongly suspected, or alive – would remain a mystery for at least another day.

That same afternoon, as the police were desperately trying to discover the location of Huelin's body, the coroner's inquest was formally opened into the death of Ann Boss. It was held at the Black Lion public house (now the Pig's Ear), 100 yards from the murder scene, on the corner of Church Street (now Old Church Street) and Paultons Street. To this day the coroners' court is the most important court in the British legal system. The inquest (originating from the word 'inquisition') was generally held in a convenient local building close to the scene of the death; this would often be a public house or a town hall. The coroner has a specific responsibility to establish where, when and why the deceased person died, but does not have the duty to identify or criminally try any suspect; that falls under the remit of the criminal court.

The inquest was opened by coroner Dr Thomas Diplock who heard evidence from several key witnesses including Henry Piper, Mrs Harriett Middleton and the officer in charge of the case, Superintendent William Fisher. Fisher supplied details of the person in custody, Walter Millar, the identification of the deceased as Ann Boss and the efforts to trace her next of kin and details of the property, belonging to the deceased, found on Millar. Superintendent Fisher also advised Dr Diplock on the current progress of the investigation into the death of Ann Boss and the search for missing landlord Elias Huelin. The inquest was adjourned, pending the completion of the police investigation, for a full coroner's inquest to take place in the near future.

Superintendent Fisher visited Millar at St George's Hospital later that evening around 8 p.m. He found Walter Millar able to talk and in good health but did not question him at this time due to Millar still being under the medical care of the hospital. The prognosis of the suspected killer was good news to the detectives. Fisher recorded in a memo to Police Commissioner Colonel Henderson that the hospital doctor had claimed that Millar 'was feigning his stupor and will probably be quite fit to be charged before a magistrate tomorrow'. A further report submitted later that evening by an officer accompanying Fisher underlined the concern that the police had yet to identify the female accomplice who made good her escape. He goes on to mention that two bricklayers should be employed the following day, if necessary, to take up the flagstones and continue with the search for Elias Huelin (National Archives MEPO 3/97).

The search at No. 24 Wellington Square was progressively being narrowed down to the back yard and garden areas of the house, but the police were baffled as there appeared to be no ground disturbance. What they needed was a break, a piece of luck. Tomorrow was Friday the thirteenth: would it be unlucky for some?

6

Friday, 13 May 1870

The following morning officers returned to No. 24 Wellington Square and continued with their search for Huelin, excavating the back yard but not as far as the flag-stoned area towards the garden wall. Two pieces of news came to the search team early that afternoon that would strengthen their resolve to find the missing man. The first, a telegram from Police Inspector Prescott, confirmed that Elias Huelin had not been seen at his farm in Navenby, Lincolnshire, for at least six weeks. This information, coupled with the tracing of witnesses such as Robert Cox, William Sansom and Thomas Walker, whose evidence had confirmed the last place Huelin was seen alive was indeed Wellington Square, convinced the team that it was highly likely Elias Huelin's body was con-cealed within the confines of this house. The search continued but no body was found.

Edward James Payne was the labourer hired by Walter Millar on Monday, 9 May to dig a ditch for drainage in the backyard of No. 24 Wellington Square and he had returned to the house several times to be paid for his work and collect his pick and shovel; he was angry that he could not locate Walter Millar. Payne, not a man to read a newspaper, heard the news everyone in Chelsea and Fulham was talking about, the murder of Ann Boss and the missing Elias Huelin, but it was not until he made the connection with No. 24 Wellington Square on Thursday night that he went to Chelsea police station and reported all that he knew. It was the break the police so desperately needed; with no corpse they would have been hard-pressed to charge Walter Millar with the murder of Elias Huelin. Payne was taken to Wellington Square; he identified to police the area where he had dug the ditch, which was now filled. The police were sceptical, as none of the flagstones appeared to have been disturbed; they questioned Payne further. Payne convinced them he was not mistaken, telling the officers that Millar insisted they not be moved. Detectives William Watts and Edward Clough lifted the flagstones and discovered recently disturbed earth which had been replaced. The body of a man fitting the description of the missing victim was unearthed in the shallow grave. The corpse was dressed in a shirt, gloves, trousers, boots and cravat, but no coat or hat. The body was removed from the grave and placed nearby in the back kitchen. The officers found a man's coat under the victim's head; one sleeve of the coat was inside out. A piece of rope was tied tightly around his neck with the knot under the right ear. Watts cut the rope away and later measured it at 11in long. A local surgeon was summoned to examine the body.

Thomas Aubrey Turner of No. 182 King's Road, Chelsea, attended the murder scene. He found the body where it had been placed following its discovery. He informed the police that Elias Huelin was a person whom he had known personally but not professionally, thus supplying positive identification of the victim. A contradiction appears in the accounts given by the doctor and Detective Watts as the doctor noted that the rope was still in position around the deceased's neck when he arrived. It is doubtful that Watts would have removed the rope before the arrival of the surgeon as this action would have compromised the surgeon's ability to provide a sound professional early judgement as to cause of death. Turner also noted that the rope was tied tightly around the neck, the knot coming under the right ear, with blood on the right side of Huelin's head emanating from a large wound. He thought that this was probably caused by a blunt instrument, corresponding with the blood found in the hat. Knowing that he would be carrying out the post-mortem in the near future, Dr Turner did not examine the head injury further at this time. The body was removed from the house and taken to the mortuary at the Chelsea workhouse on nearby Arthur Street (now Dovehouse Street) where it would remain until the following day's post-mortem examination.

Both houses, where such ghastly acts of violence had taken place, were cordoned off by the police. Superintendent Fisher and his team still had a lot of work to do. Why were two much-loved and respected members of the Chelsea community killed? What was the motive that drove the killer or killers to use such force? And in the case of Elias Huelin, what and where was the murder weapon?

The police were now anxious to place Walter Millar in front of the police court. The public outcry against such unspeakable crimes in the affluent areas of Chelsea and Fulham, whipped up by an ever-growing media free-for-all, demanded tangible progress, and that progress would be the appearance of the suspect Walter Millar in front of a magistrate, charged with these despicable crimes. Neither the public nor the media had any comprehension of the restraints the police were under, a fact underlined by the reluctance of the medical staff at St George's Hospital to release Millar back into the custody of the police. Fisher explains his frustrations in a memo dated 13 May 1870, and timed at 11.25 a.m.: 'Hospital authorities cannot say till 1 p.m. whether prisoner Millar can be removed' (National Archives MEPO 3/97).

Walter Millar was, at last, transported by Inspector Pitt Tarlton and Police Sergeant John Large from St George's Hospital to Westminster Police Court in Rochester Row, SW1, later that Friday afternoon. Before his appearance at the specially convened court he was taken to the cell complex where he was formally charged by Inspector Tarlton with 'Feloniously killing and slaying Ann Boss at 15 Paultons Square, King's Road, Chelsea'. Millar made no reply to the charge.

'Do you understand the charge made against you?' Tarlton asked the prisoner.

'You said something about murder,' Millar replied in a rare recorded answer. Tarlton repeated the charge to Millar who replied, 'I will say nothing now'. A short time later, the fact that the body of Elias Huelin had been discovered was passed to Inspector Tarlton and Millar was charged, on the basis of the circumstantial evidence of Edward Payne, with the wilful murder of Elias Huelin at No. 24 Wellington Square, Chelsea.

Walter Millar appeared in front of stipendiary magistrate Mr Selfe charged with two counts of wilful murder. It was the first occasion that the general public were given an insight into the events that had occurred and, more interestingly, into the man who was accused of committing them. The 31-year-old alleged murderer was described as:

A tall powerfully built man of a rough and sullen and forbidding aspect. He was dressed in his working clothes, wore no necktie, and seemed dead to, rather than actively sensible of, the position in which he stood. At the time it was tolerably evident that he was still to some extent under the soporific influence of the laudanum which he had taken on arrest.

The Daily Telegraph, 14 May 1870

Superintendent Fisher appeared on behalf of the prosecution, stating that the police were not in a position to proceed with the second murder charge (that of Elias Huelin) due to the lack of time since the discovery of the body and the impending post-mortem examination the following morning.

The magistrate called for evidence from Mrs Harriett Middleton, who gave her account from the time she received a visit from the prisoner dressed as a French gentleman at her address on the night of Monday, 9 May, until the discovery and identification of the body of Ann Boss at No. 15 Paultons Square on Wednesday, 11 May. Walter Millar sat silently listening to the damning evidence being given against him. Mr Selfe asked the prisoner if he wished to make any comment or ask the witness any questions. Millar cleared his throat before answering in the negative. Further evidence was heard from Henry Piper and Dr Henry Thomas Ryder.

Millar refrained from asking any questions of the witnesses at this hearing and he was not represented by any defence solicitor at this early stage. Reporters present in the courtroom give us an insight into the demeanour of the prisoner who had, at least towards the end of this hearing, come to terms with the situation in which he found himself:

In the course of his examination he so nearly fainted that the magistrate ordered him to be provided with a chair, and during the remainder of the proceedings he sat in the dock. He was tightly handcuffed, a kind of precaution that is nowadays quite unusual, but which is probably fully justifiable by the desperate character of the individual.

The Daily Telegraph, 14 May 1870

The magistrate, Mr Selfe, adjourned the case until the following day in order for the police to progress their enquiries into the death of Elias Huelin. There was no question of Walter Millar being allowed bail and he was transferred by taxi with a police guard to the house of detention. The magistrate ordered that a post-mortem on Ann Boss was unnecessary, as the cause of death was clear.

Following her arrest for being drunk and disorderly in the early hours of Thursday, 12 May and her subsequent caution from Magistrate Selfe later the same day, Elizabeth Green was released. However, this was not to be her last role in this sordid affair. A few hours after Walter Millar had been remanded in custody, Green was in the vicinity of her home on St Anne Street, Westminster, when a sharp-eyed police officer, Inspector Humphrys, having seen Walter Millar at the earlier court hearing, recognised Elizabeth Green as a woman he had seen in the company of Millar on Wednesday, 11 May. He was quite sure it was the same lady; he remembered the flaming colours of the skirt Millar bought her, which she was still wearing. Inspector Humphrys arrested Elizabeth Green on suspicion of the murder of Ann Boss and she was transferred to Chelsea police station for questioning.

Later, during her interrogation, Green denied any role in the murder of Ann Boss and claimed she had no knowledge of the murder before, or on her arrival, at No. 15 Paultons Square, Chelsea. Her story bore a sense of truth regarding meeting Walter Millar in the West End where she had clothes and alcohol bought for her; much of this recollection was confirmed by Inspector Humphrys. She also stated that upon her arrival at the house she was already heavily intoxicated, which only increased with the offer of another drink, which consequently led to her refusal of a second. She said that she could not remember going down to the back kitchen or seeing any box therein. Her next recollection was being arrested in the early hours of Thursday morning and appearing before the magistrate. A statement was taken from her as a witness for the prosecution, to be used against Walter Millar at his trial.

7

SATURDAY, 14 MAY 1870

T he arrival of the weekend sent the levels of interest in the murders soaring as graphic details of the crimes appeared in nearly every newspaper both in the capital and nationally. The crowds were out in force, all approaches to Westminster Police Court in Rochester Row were lined with an unruly agitated presence and an undercurrent of violence oozed from onlookers waiting for a chance to vent their anger and disgust at the man responsible (they believed) for these horrendous murders. Walter Millar was brought to the court from the house of detention by taxi, accompanied by a police guard; he was heavily secured in irons as the police feared that he might take his own life.

The prosecution case was presented by Superintendent Fisher (the police prosecuted cases in magistrates' court until the introduction of the Crown Prosecution Service in the mid 1980s). Mr Selfe had called for further evidence of identification and Elizabeth Green (who was brought from Chelsea police station) was asked if she could identify the person she had met in the West End who had bought her food and clothes and taken her back to No. 15 Paultons Square that same night. She looked around the court at everybody but the defendant. When she did make eye-contact with Millar, who was standing in the dock looking at her with a degree of intensity, she fainted. On her revival, she became hysterical when asked to give her evidence and was removed from the court.

Police Constable Coles produced for the court the title deeds covered in blood which had been found on Walter Millar on the night of his arrest. Evidence was then given by Dr Thomas Aubrey Turner. The court, including those members of the general public who were lucky enough to have gained entry into the small public gallery, fell silent and listened intently to every word uttered by the medical practitioner. He described in graphic detail the findings of his post-mortem examination carried out on Friday night at the Chelsea workhouse. His first revelation was that Elias Huelin was not strangled by the rope tied around his neck. In his professional opinion, it was attached after death and probably used to drag the corpulent victim from the place of death and probable concealment, in the back kitchen, to the place of burial in the back yard. He continued:

> I found a wound to the left side of the head – the temple – as if from a heavy blow. At the back of the neck or rather the base of the skull there were two holes scarcely as large as peas and on pressing the area of these injuries parts of the brain protruded.

He waited for the gasps from the public gallery to subside, enjoying the moment, before continuing: 'There were no other external marks of violence. The holes I have mentioned were sufficient to account for death; the cause of which was a fracture to the base of the skull.'

Millar stood throughout the doctor's evidence, staring at a fixed point in front of him, displaying no emotion. Turner continued:

> I do not think such an instrument as a pickaxe would have produced the holes. They were so excessively small that it must have been a very sharp implement; much sharper than the pick. The holes broke into the brain cells (through the skull) at the back of the ear.

The next witness called by Superintendent Fisher was the long-term friend of both the victims, Mr John Carter. Carter told the court that earlier that morning he had been taken to the Chelsea workhouse mortuary where he identified the bodies of both Ann Boss and Elias Huelin. Carter was shown a pair of boots, a hat (described to the court as a clerical hat) and a pair of spectacles, all taken from the prisoner at the time of his arrest. Carter identified that all once belonged to Elias Huelin. Carter qualified his statement by saying Huelin had mentioned to Carter on Friday, 6 May – three days before the murder – that he had lost his glasses.

Elizabeth Green was returned to the court at the insistence of the magistrate (who was probably quite frustrated that he had been unaware of her involvement in this case when she had appeared in front of him on the Thursday morning for drunkenness) who wished to discover her role in this case. The *London Daily News* 12 May described the terrified young woman: 'She presented an idiotic appearance, and is paralysed down on the left side; she, however, gave her evidence very well.'

Green stated that she and her husband Edward lived at No. 27 St Anne Street in Westminster. She gave her account of meeting the prisoner near Windmill Street on the afternoon of Wednesday, 11 May. She said that he bought her some food and drink in a public house followed by some clothes. She was then asked specific questions by the magistrate:

'Did you see a van or anybody at the door [of No. 15 Paultons Square]?'

'No.'

'Were you not in the house on the landing and the prisoner followed you upstairs?'

'No. I never saw anybody, I am sure.'

'It appears he took her to a good many public houses,' Superintendent Fisher intervened, 'so that may account for her forgetfulness of what took place in the house.'

'I know,' rebuked the magistrate; 'she was charged before me with being drunk and incapable the next morning, and I let her go, on the promise she would keep from drink and go to Cambridgeshire where she came from.'

'I will never transgress again,' Green volunteered, keeping her eyes focused on the bench and avoiding the stare of the prisoner.

'It's a pity you came to London,' Selfe commented.

'I believe he bought you some clothes?' Fisher asked.

'Yes, he bought me this hat and dress, jacket, boots and stays; he changed silver, and as he did so gave me the coppers.'

Walter Millar was remanded in custody to appear a week later in order that the coroner's inquests into the deaths of the two victims could be finalised.

The Victorians were a ghoulish breed, fascinated by death, and as such the courts and crime scenes played host to huge crowds, all of them hoping to catch a sight of a location or person they had been following in the media. Wellington and Paultons squares were mobbed by people from near and far. This show of entertainment was one that could not be missed (the last public execution had taken place in England in 1868, when terrorist Michael Barrett was hanged outside Newgate

Prison in front of a crowd of over 20,000 people). The local residents, in particular those living in Wellington Square, were extremely concerned, fearing mayhem and rioting over the weekend. A letter was received at Scotland Yard addressed to the Commissioner, Colonel Edmund Henderson:

Sir,

We the undersigned inhabitants of Wellington Square beg respect-fully to request that you will order a sufficient police force on duty on Sunday (15 May 1870) to prevent the assembling of 'Roughs' usually witnessed on these occasions and this will save us the annoyance we may otherwise be subject to and you will greatly oblige.

Sir

Your servants

(National Archives MEPO 3/97)

The letter was signed by fifteen residents of Wellington Square. The request was passed to the Superintendent in charge of 'B' division for 'immediate' action. There were necessary numbers of police deployed to Wellington and Paultons Squares over the next few days, avoiding any obstruction to the daily lives of those residents living there.

8

MONDAY,
16 MAY 1870

The inquest into the death of Elias Huelin was opened by Dr Thomas Diplock, the coroner for West Middlesex, in the boardroom of the Chelsea workhouse in Arthur Street. Diplock was an extremely experienced coroner who covered a huge area of London and who would, in the future, conduct the inquests of several victims of 'Jack the Ripper' in 1888.

A jury of twenty-one gentlemen and tradesmen, all local to the Chelsea area, were sworn in and took the short walk to the workhouse mortuary (or dead-house, as reported in the *London Daily News* on 17 May) in order to view the corpse of Elias Huelin and in particular the injuries inflicted. They discovered that the body was not badly disfigured; notable injuries were a cut under the left eye and two small holes on the left side of the skull. The coroner and the jury were then taken to No. 24 Wellington Square to examine the scene of the murder. They were shown the trench in which the late Elias Huelin was discovered and the room in the basement, the probable scene of his murder. This was useful for the jurors and a method which is often used today before trials and inquests; photographic evidence is often produced during an inquest or trial but jurors can relate to witnesses' evidence with greater clarity if they have seen the relevant locations themselves.

A number of witnesses were called whose evidence has already been examined. Mr John Carter, in addition to his previous accounts, added that the deceased was 84 years old and was in very good pecuniary circumstances.

Detective William Watts was asked for more specific details about the discovery of the body. He recalled:

In the afternoon of Friday [13 May] in consequence of something said by Payne [his account of digging the drain for Millar] a large stone was removed from the floor of the back water closet and cleared away the soil to a depth of about 3 feet 8 inches. At about half-past two I saw a human arm in the earth, with a glove and a mitten on the hand, and on removing more of the soil came to the head and the rest of the body which was lying slightly on its left side with the right arm thrown over the throat and neck. Nearly the whole of the body was under the foundation of the water closet and we had to remove the bricks to get him out. He was in his shirt sleeves and a piece of rope was tied around his neck very tightly. There was no drain in that direction; the hole evidently had been dug for the purpose for which it was used.

The silent courtroom echoed his words as the jury listened to the officer's account. Watts continued:

We found the coat of the deceased under where the body lay. The hole and the premises were searched for any weapon or implement with which the murder might have been committed but found nothing but a shovel and a pick.

Doctor Aubrey Turner, who had carried out the post-mortem on Elias Huelin, was next to give evidence to the jury; it differed little from that which he gave at the police court a few days earlier apart from one significant aspect, the murder weapon. Dr Diplock asked the witness if he had any notion about the sort of instrument used to inflict such unusual injuries. Turner suggested that, in his opinion, the most likely instrument would have been a slater's hammer.

The court murmured with excitement as the next witness was called; an unhealthy-looking, apprehensive 18 year old shuffled into the witness box looking nervously around the wood-panelled room, surprised at the reaction he appeared to have created.

'Can you tell us your name, sir?' Dr Diplock enquired.

'Edward Huelin. I am the nephew of the late Elias Huelin and now live at No. 15 Paultons Square, Chelsea.'

'Can you tell us the relationship, as far as you are aware, between your uncle and that of the defendant, Walter Millar?'

'Yes, Millar was a tenant of my uncle's at Seymour Place, next to where my uncle formerly lived. I called upon him for rent in March.' Edward Huelin went on to explain that he would often go out and collect rent on his uncle's behalf. He was then asked to identify certain articles that had been found on the prisoner when he had been arrested and during the subsequent search of his home address.

'I can identify the spectacles, the silver pencil case and the rent book found on the prisoner, Millar, as property belonging to my uncle. The rent book, having kept it myself, all but the first page.'

'When did you discover that your uncle had been murdered?'

'I have been very ill,' Huelin replied, 'I was in Lincolnshire when the murder was committed. I first heard of the murder on Thursday. I was expecting my uncle down to visit me every day. He wrote to me on 24 April, saying he was coming.'

John Carter was recalled to identify the boots which Millar had been wearing at Chelsea police station following his arrest, the overcoat that he had discarded during the chase prior to his arrest, the hat that had been found during the search of No. 24 Wellington Square and the spectacles which Elias Huelin had told the witness he had lost, which were also found on the prisoner. The inquest was then adjourned until later in the week.

Dr Diplock then travelled the short distance from the Chelsea workhouse to the Black Lion public house in Paultons Street to resume the inquest into the death of the other victim, Ann Boss.

The second day of the hearing opened with questions about the search of No. 15 Paultons Square on the night of Monday, 9 May following the report of the premises being insecure by Samuel Stainsby and the degree of seriousness with which the police had treated the situation. Superintendent Fisher defended his officer's actions, stating that:

> The police could not take any active steps till a felony had been proved to have taken place, and with respect to Mr Carter [who appears to be the person causing the debate], he on Tuesday [10th May] told the police that he believed that it was all right; and Mr Carter appeared to be Mr Huelin's most intimate friend.

John Hunt, the keeper of Paultons Square, re-affirmed the convincing nature of Walter Millar's disguise when he described seeing Millar before the murders took place with his whiskers and seeing him since without them and the difficulty he believed he would have in recognising him.

Other witnesses were also heard, mostly re-confirming previously examined evidence. The only witness to offer something new to the proceedings was Samuel Stainsby, who had alerted the police to the insecure property in which the body of Ann Boss lay. He offered a more robust version of his suspicions, stating that he was sure something was seriously wrong and that the police could have done more to rectify the situation (probably alluding to the fact that they failed to search the box which concealed the body). He also offered accounts, of little more than idle gossip, which he and his family had overheard. Dr Diplock pointed out to the witness that he could not give evidence of anything he had not heard himself (hearsay evidence) as that would not be admissible. The jury seemed to become impatient with this ruling, stating, 'There is no imputation against anybody else.' Dr Diplock ignored their representations, aware of the rules of evidence and the serious complications such evidence could cause at a future criminal trial.

After hearing all the available evidence, the coroner began his summing up of the facts to the jury. He concluded by stating:

> That last Thursday [12 May] there were certain reasons for suspecting that another man had been concerned in the murder, but evidence points solely to the prisoner, his object apparently being to possess himself of property in the house where the deceased resided. In reference to the Middletons, there did not seem to be anything to connect them with the crime of murder. There have, however, been certain questions put to ascertain whether or not they were accomplices after the fact for the purpose of robbery [dealt with in a later chapter]. I do not think there was anything to show that. They appeared to have both been deceived by the prisoner's disguise. They had told the same story throughout the case, and their evidence had not been shaken, but strengthened in part by other evidence given.

The jury was asked to retire and consider their verdicts. Just five minutes had elapsed when the jury returned their verdict of 'Wilful Murder'. The jury also expressed their approval to the coroner of the actions of van proprietor Henry Piper in apprehending the main suspect for the murder, Walter Millar, and suggested that Piper be deserving of some reward from the county.

9

WEDNESDAY, 18 MAY 1870

With the inquest verdict into the death of Ann Boss final-ised and the likelihood of a similar outcome at the inquest into the death of Elias Huelin, the bodies of the deceased were released to their families for burial. The funeral possession wound its way from the mortuary at the Chelsea workhouse, north to the Fulham Road, passing Seymour Place – the former home of Elias Huelin and Ann Boss and the present home of Walter Millar's family – and into the Brompton Cemetery where Huelin had spent his last working days.

Brompton cemetery was opened in 1840 as one of the 'Magnificent Seven' cemeteries created in countryside sur-rounding London to relieve the appalling overcrowding in city churchyards. The Metropolitan Internments Act of 1850 prohibited the burial of the dead in urban churchyards and gave government the power to compulsory-purchase privately owned cemeteries; Brompton became the first and only cemetery to be nationalised following its sale in 1852. Today, the cemetery buildings, including the chapel with which Elias

Huelin would have been so familiar, and twenty-eight of its monuments are Grade II listed and the cemetery is administered and maintained by the Royal Parks.

The families of the deceased were represented by Ann Boss's two sisters, Charlotte and one unnamed, and her brother-in-law, and Elias Huelin's two nephews: Edward, who was now back living in his uncle's house in Paultons Square, and Elias who had travelled to London from Jersey. The victim's friends included John Carter and the solicitor for the Huelin family, Mr Richard Wright. On arrival at the graveside, the party were met by a significant group of mourners, numbering in excess of sixty. The service was carried out by Rev. Dr Wilson, a close friend of the deceased. The strain was too much for one of the Boss sisters, who fainted by the graveside. She was taken into the nearby vestry where she was tended to with the sensitivity needed at such a distressing time. Huelin and his loyal housekeeper Ann Boss were buried in the same grave near to the south wall of the cemetery.

The coroner, Dr Diplock, returned following the funeral to the Chelsea workhouse to resume the inquest into the death of Elias Huelin. The public's interest in the case had waned somewhat since the funerals this morning, as only those directly involved with the inquest attended the hearing. However, an anonymous letter was handed to and read by the coroner. The letter was addressed to Samuel Stainsby at No. 14 Paultons Square, Chelsea, questioning Stainsby's motives for entering No. 15 on the night of the 9 May:

Mr, I have read your voluntary evidence in today's paper from which I draw my own conclusion. Now what right had you to suspect something was wrong and to search the house by entering the backdoor? I judge after your hearing of the diabolical affair, and happening to know the unfortunate Mr Huelin and Mrs Goss [*sic*], you like such busy fools, thought you might make yourself prominent. Beware how you tamper with the life of a fellow creature; and be not too ready to give evidence founded entirely on your own ideas, with the object of making yourself notorious. You will be well watched in this matter.

A Friend at Present.

The letter was postmarked London SE and dated 'May 17, '70' (National Archives MEPO 3/97). The coroner disregarded the letter as having no evidential value. However, Samuel Stainsby did receive substantial criticism from both Chelsea residents and the media for his perceived inaction on that Monday night; however, by the time he entered the house both victims were dead and there was little more he could have achieved.

Other witnesses attended and gave evidence (previously mentioned) to the jury, who were very attentive and often questioned witnesses in order to clarify points made during their accounts. Dr Diplock summed up the case to the jury, who returned their verdict of 'Wilful Murder' in very quick time.

Central criminal court, the 'Old Bailey'. (G. Pilkington)

No. 14 (home of Samuel Stainsby) and No. 15 (home of Elias Huelin and Ann Boss), Paultons Square, Chelsea. (G. Pilkington)

Former location of Chelsea workhouse around 1870, now Dovehouse Street.
(G. Pilkington)

Chelsea workhouse, Arthur Street, Chelsea (now Dovehouse Street), in around 1870. (Reproduced by kind permission of the Royal Borough of Kensington and Chelsea Libraries Service)

Old Bailey dictum and scales of justice. (G. Pilkington)

Central gardens, Paultons Square. (G. Pilkington)

Original Paultons Square sign. (G. Pilkington)

The Pig's Ear public house, formerly the Black Lion, location of the inquest into Ann Boss's death. (G. Pilkington)

The Black Lion public house in around 1870. (Reproduced by kind permission of the Royal Borough of Kensington and Chelsea Libraries Services)

No. 24 Wellington Square, the location of Elias Huelin's murder. (G. Pilkington)

Borough of Chelsea
WELLINGTON SQ.

Borough of Chelsea: Wellington Square sign. (G. Pilkington)

Chelsea police station, King's Road, around 1870. (Reproduced by kind permission of Julian Jephcote)

Former St George's hospital, Hyde Park Corner, where Millar was treated. (Author's collection)

French Protestant church, Soho Square, where Elias Huelin was a member of the clergy. (Author's collection)

Central gardens, Wellington Square, laid out in the 1830s. (G. Pilkington)

Lombard Street, Chelsea, around 1870: the scene of Walter Millar's arrest. (Reproduced by kind permission of the Royal Borough of Kensington and Chelsea Libraries Services)

King's Road junction with Paultons Square, around 1870: the location Piper first reported his suspicions to police. (Reproduced by kind permission of the Royal Borough of Kensington and Chelsea Libraries Services)

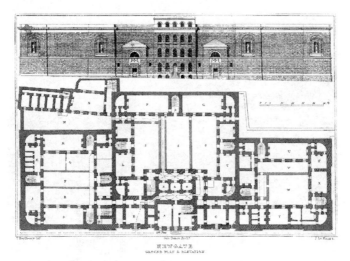

Plan of Newgate prison. (THP)

Newgate Street with Newgate prison on the right. (THP)

Newgate prison just before its demolition. (THP)

The Central Criminal Court (or the 'Old Bailey') with Newgate Prison in the distance. (THP)

Metropolitan Police memo from Inspector Prescott reporting that Elias Huelin had never arrived at Navenby Farm in Lincolnshire. (National Archives MEPO/3/97)

Metropolitan Police.

COMMISSIONER'S OFFICE,

13th day of May 1870

Telegram received from *Col. Fearon B.*

for *Col. Henderson*

at *8.55* o'clock *p.* m.

The dead Body of the Revd Mr

Huelin has been found at 24 Wellington
Square, Chelsea. The Prisoner is now
at Westminster Police Court. going
before the Magistrate

J. E. Thompson

¹ Signature and rank of Officer who receives the Message.

Metropolitan Police memo reporting the discovery of Elias Huelin's body in Wellington Square and noting that the prisoner is due to appear at Westminster police court. (National Archives MEPO/3/97)

Sir,

The above is a drawing of a tool used by slaters – might it not have been used by the Murderer

The likely 'murder weapon', a slater's tool, as suggested by anonymous letter. (National Archives MEPO/3/97)

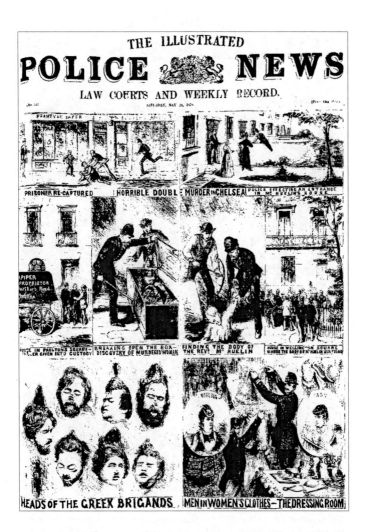

Police Illustrated News reporting the double murder in Chelsea. (Images copyright The British Library Board. All rights reserved. Reproduced by kind permission of Brightsolid Newspaper Archives Ltd)

Police Illustrated News reporting the Westminster police court appearance of
Walter Millar and witnesses, 28 May 1870. (Images copyright The British
Library Board. All rights reserved. Reproduced by kind permission of Brightsolid
Newspaper Archives Ltd)

10

Friday, 20 May 1870

Public interest reignited as Walter Millar arrived early at Westminster Police Court; this would be the last appearance of the charged man at the lower court. Mr Selfe, the chief magistrate, who had been in charge of the case since the start of the prosecution, was the examining official. Today, it was the responsibility of the court to examine the evidence on which the prosecution would base their case at the crown court trial. Due to the seriousness of the charges, the location for the trial would be the Central Criminal Court located at the Old Bailey, EC4.

Walter Millar was represented at these proceedings by an attorney who could challenge, on behalf of his client, evidence given by the witnesses in order to try and persuade the court that a *Prima facie* case (a Latin term which means 'on first examination', or that a matter seems to be evident) had not been proven. Walter Millar's legal representative was Mr Bury Hutchinson, who, as noted by the *London Daily News*, was being instructed by the Society for the Abolition

of Capital Punishment. During the reign of Queen Victoria
(1837–1901) the number of offences for which capital punishment could be exercised were reduced so that only murder
remained. Yet there were a growing number of Victorians who
were determined to eradicate the death penalty altogether;
societies, such as the Abolition of Capital Punishment, were
a prominent voice against what they perceived to be 'murder
by the state'. Not only did they force the issue into the public
arena through media and public meetings but, as in this case,
they funded legal representation for those facing the death
sentence. Of course their efforts were in vain as it would be
another ninety-five years until the Murder (Abolition of the
Death Penalty) Act 1965 became law.

Again the police were represented by the officer in charge
of the investigation, Superintendent Fisher. We have heard the
majority of the evidence given by the witnesses in this case, but
it is of added value to examine the questions put to the witnesses
by Fisher and by Millar's solicitor, Bury Hutchinson. Harriett
Sibley was a friend of the Millars and gave her account of seeing
Walter Millar on the Monday afternoon when he returned
home in his work clothes, changing into a clean shirt, ironed
by his wife, before leaving the house stating he was going to
Hornsey in North London regarding work prospects. It was, of
course, alleged by the prosecution that by this time Millar had
already murdered both Ann Boss and Elias Huelin. The question by Hutchinson to the witness was an obvious one, if the
defendent had been involved in the commission of these savage
crimes only hours earlier, as the prosecution were alleging:

'Did you notice anything different in the behaviour of
Walter Millar?'

'He was not disturbed in his mind or disturbed that I noticed,'
Mrs Sibley replied, confidently.

Frederick Charles Vince, the gas worker approached by Millar in Sands End and asked if he wished to earn 'a shilling or two' for moving a box, was questioned by Superintendent Fisher as to what time he first saw Millar that afternoon [Tuesday, 10 May].

'I saw him about two o'clock at first that day.'

'When you went to Paultons Square with the defendant did you see which house he entered before leaving you with the instructions to get your cart and return to the square?'

'I saw the prisoner go into a house, I could not see which one,' replied Vince.

Rebecca Evans – the lady who had rented property from Huelin and attempted to return the key on the afternoon of Monday, 9 May about 4 p.m. – when questioned further about what she had seen on that first visit remembered that she had noticed Huelin's small dog locked out of the house on the doorstep.

Dr Francis Godrich was the first professional witness to give evidence at the committal hearing. He recalled the circumstances under which he had been called out to Chelsea police station on Wednesday, 11 May; this is a testimony worth revisiting as he gives significant additional evidence about the physical health of the prisoner on the night of his arrest:

I was called to Chelsea police station about half past ten on Wednesday night to attend the prisoner, who, they [the police] said had taken poison. I spoke in both English and French to him [Millar] and he did not answer. His eyes were shut, but there was motion of the limbs. The pupils were dilatable and normal, and the pulse was regular. I gave him an emetic and part of the [resulting] vomit I kept for chemical analysis. I received from Inspector Tarlton a broken bottle with an undrawn cork wedged tightly in the broken neck; it had not been removed. I washed the bottle and the paper that enveloped it,

and found on analysis of the water, that it contained meconic acid and
morphia, the actual constituents of Laudanum. In the vomited matter
I found no poison, and I believed, and do now, that the prisoner was
hamming; I only found the Zinc I had given in the emetic. I traced
by the label and found where the stuff had been bought and found he
had bought two-penny worth, or about 70 drops.

Mr Selfe asked the witness what effect such a dose would have
had on a person. Godrich replied, 'That would not destroy life,'
and added, 'I think he was conscious all the time, but mentally
depressed by fear and drink.'

Dr Thomas Aubrey Turner, who had carried out the post-
mortem on Elias Huelin, added to his evidence that he had
been asked to examine some marks on the wall of the house
at No. 24 Wellington Square, under the stairs, about a yard off
the ground. He continued: 'I found stains of human blood, such
as would proceed from the head of a body placed in a sitting
position against the wall.' He continued, in order to clarify:
'They were large stains and were under the stairs and a cupboard.'
Mrs Harriett Middleton was recalled by Hutchinson in relation
to identification issues and when questioned replied:

I knew the prisoner [as Walter Millar] was no relative of Mr Huelin,
and knew he was not a Frenchman, but he was very different in fine
clothes with spectacles, his whiskers shaved off and speaking like
a foreigner, than he was in his working clothes. I am rather short-
sighted and he never looked me fair in the face, but turned his head.

Following the completion of the prosecution evidence (the prisoner at this period in history had no right to be heard; this will
be explored in a later chapter), Mr Selfe cautioned Walter
Millar on both charges and asked if he had anything to say.

'I am not guilty.' Walter Millar replied, simply.

Selfe looked at the prisoner and declared: 'You are committed to take your trial at the Old Bailey for the wilful murder of Elias Huelin and Ann Boss.' The *London Daily News* reports that he was allowed a visit from his wife before being removed from the court amid the violent and menacing cries from a hostile crowd.

11

The Trial:
Day One

Wednesday, 13 July 1870

We have so far heard from all the main protagonists in this tale of wicked violence and greed. But the true test of any witness and the reliability of their evidence can only be examined in a court of law in front of a judge and jury. It is important to remember that the basis of English law is founded on the concept that one is innocent until proven guilty; Millar may already have been found guilty by the press and to some degree by the coroner's court, but only one court mattered, the one in which he was now to be tried. By using the contemporary accounts of the day, we can now examine the strength and weaknesses of the prosecution's case and the jury's verdict; would Walter Millar convince a jury that he was innocent of wilful murder or would he hang from the gallows?

The trial of the Crown versus Walter Millar began at the Central Criminal Court (often referred to as 'The Old Bailey') on 13 July 1870. The jury was made up of twelve male jurors who were presided over by the trial judge. Although the defendant was represented at the trial by his own barrister, English law at this time had not progressed to allowing the defendant to give evidence of his account from the witness box; this right would not be introduced into the English legal system until the 1880s. Trial by jury is nearly as old as the English legal system itself; the first trial involving a jury in a criminal matter took place during the reign of Henry II in 1168 when the defendant, Benedict Graymond, was tried and convicted by a jury for murder.

The procedural order of a criminal trial in England has changed little over the last 200 years or so. The defendant would have the indictment read to him and was then asked to enter a plea of guilty or not guilty to each charge on the indictment. This would be followed by the prosecution counsel opening the case against the defendant and then calling witnesses to provide enough reliable evidence to prove the defendant's guilt beyond any reasonable doubt. The onus of proof in 1870 is the same as it is today: the prosecution must prove the case; the defendant does not have to prove their innocence. Each of the prosecution witnesses gives their evidence from their recollection (having been allowed to read any written statement given by them before the commencement of their evidence). Each witness will be cross-examined by the defence barrister; this will include questions about any discrepancies in a witness's account in relation to any previous account given in statement form or when examined at committal proceedings or at the police court, the inquest or in relation to another's evidence. These all provide chances to challenge the validity of the account from the defendant's point of view. Then the prosecution is given another chance to clear up any ambiguities that have arisen from the cross-examination. Finally, the judge himself may well want to ask questions of the witness.

Since the 1880s (as previously mentioned) the defendant could choose whether to give evidence from the witness box or not; this right was not available to Walter Millar in 1870. Both the prosecution and the defence would then be allowed to 'sum up' their respective cases as to the defendant's guilt or innocence. This would be followed by the judge's summing up in which he would direct the jury with regard to the law and reflect on the facts of the case, as given in evidence, before sending them out to decide upon their verdict. Another difference between 1870 and present day is the disclosure, by the prosecution, of any evidence on which they rely to the defence. Indeed, this requirement did not enter English law until the introduction of the Criminal Procedures and Investigation Act of 1996.

The indictment on which Walter Millar was to be tried contained only one charge of wilful murder – that of Elias Huelin. Lord Chief Justice Cockburn was the judge and had decided, probably after the representations from both the prosecution and defence counsels, that the murders were quite separate acts and that they should be tried as such; however, it was inevitable that evidence would be introduced into the trial that referred to the murder of housekeeper Ann Boss. Barristers for the Crown were Mr Poland and Mr Beasley and for Walter Millar's defence, Mr Collins and Mr St Aubyn.

In order to avoid any repetition of witness accounts I have, at times, summarised answers to questions raised by the judge and in cross-examination by the defendant's barrister, unless the questions asked and the answers given shine light on facts that had not previously been unearthed or are of such significance they warrant re-examination.

Mr Poland opened the case to the court, giving an explanation for the decision to try the defendant only on the murder of Elias Huelin, as reported in the *London Daily News* (14 July 1870):

> At the Central Criminal Court yesterday before the Lord Chief Justice, Walter Millar, 31, a respectable looking man described as a plasterer, was placed at the bar to take his trial upon two charges of wilful murder – namely for the murder of the Rev Elias Huelin and the murder of his housekeeper Ann Boss.
>
> The prisoner was put upon trial for the murder of Mr Huelin.
>
> Mr Poland briefly opened the case for the prosecution observing that he considered the best course was to give a statement of the evidence he proposed to give in support of the charge; and he said at the same time that although the prisoner was only put upon his trial for one murder, it would be impossible to conceal from the jury that two murders had, in point of fact, been committed and that the prisoner was the author of both murders. He then detailed the facts, and said there could be no doubt that the prisoner had deliberately planned both murders, and carried them out with utmost coolness and deliberation.

The court was packed with members of the deceased's family and members of the general public who had queued from early morning to secure a spot in a limited public gallery. The press were present, recording every spoken word. This was the trial of the time, one of national notoriety, reported throughout the nation from Bournemouth up to Glasgow via Birmingham, Sheffield and every major city in the United Kingdom.

The prosecution presented the evidence to the jury in chronological order to enable them to follow the facts in logical form. The first witness to be called by the prosecution was Robert Cox, who knew Elias Huelin fairly well from his days as a clergyman and who had been present in Wellington Square on the morning of Monday, 9 May 1870, about 11 a.m. Robert Cox gave his evidence to the jury and answered questions by the prosecution before being offered to the defence for the purpose of cross-examination. The witness was questioned by the defence about how long he had known Elias Huelin; Cox stated that he had known him for many years. In answer to other questions he replied that he did not know Huelin's family or where he had come from, that Huelin did not speak exactly with a foreign accent but did have a slight defect in his speech and that he was a very aged man.

Cox was followed into the witness box by William Sansom who also saw Huelin in Wellington Square that same morning, having first seen him alight from an omnibus on King's Road. Sansom noted that Huelin was dressed differently to his usual appearance, wearing a new suit of clothes and a hat, and that he had no pet dog with him, which was out of character. Sansom was asked by the defence if he had been acquainted with the deceased, to which he replied, 'Not acquainted exactly, but I have known him for some years past.' He was asked, in his opinion, 'What distance is Wellington Square from Paultons Square?' Sansom estimated the distance to be in the region of about half a mile.

The third witness, Thomas Humble Walker, explained that he had seen Huelin on the steps of No. 24 Wellington Square on Monday morning at approximately 11.15 a.m. During his cross-examination it was highlighted by the defence that Walker had not actually seen Huelin enter the property that morning. Thomas Walker agreed but added: 'He was going up the steps as a man would that was going into a house.'

The investigation into these horrendous murders had been reported throughout national and local newspapers in great detail and the witnesses who were involved in the events leading up to the murders, unknowingly assisting Walter Millar in his plot, became household names. Lifelike illustrations of the witnesses appeared in publications. The *Illustrated Police News* offered such illustrations in their newspaper of witnesses who had already appeared and given their evidence in the police court and at the coroner's inquests. So when Edward James Payne was called by the prosecution, an excited buzz spread across the courtroom, a realisation that the first witness of substance was about to reveal all to those present. Payne carefully, with great attention to detail, explained his recollection of his significant role in this ghastly affair, mesmerising the jury as he recalled meeting Walter Millar, a man he had known as a plasterer, at the Admiral Keppel public house on Brompton Road, in the early afternoon of Monday, 9 May. He explained about the job offer to lift a drain, the journey to No. 24 Wellington Square, where he dug a hole 3ft deep and about 7ft long, avoiding all the flagstones, in a very specific location as instructed by Millar. He recalled that he had left his tools in the kitchen area and was told to return the following morning to fit the pipes and finish the job off. He complied with Millar's request, only to find the property empty and that he was unable to gain entry. He claimed that he visited the house on several more occasions over the next couple of days with the same result.

Payne became aware on the Friday (13 May) of the disappearance of Elias Huelin and that his housekeeper, Ann Boss, had been found murdered in a house in Paultons Square. Payne knew that the police were searching the house in which he had been working for the body of the now presumed dead former reverend. He reported his suspicion to the police at Chelsea police station, before being escorted to No. 24 Wellington Square where several police officers were searching the premises, in particular the rear yard and garden. Payne pointed out to the police where he had dug his hole and saw that it had been filled in with the spoil he had removed. After being proven correct with the discovery of a decomposing body, he assisted the police with the removal of the mud-covered corpse of Elias Huelin from the newly dug grave. The following day, Payne attended Westminster Police Court and provided a crucial piece of identification evidence, the link between Millar and the location in which the deceased was unearthed.

This continuity of evidence was tightening the rope around Walter Millar's neck. Payne confirmed to the court and the jury that the man who stood before him with his whiskers shaved off and a moustache dyed a darker colour than before was the man whom he had known for three years as Walter Millar and, crucially, that he was the man who had employed him and was present when he dug the drain hole in which the deceased had been found.

It appears that during the cross-examination the defence did not dispute the identification evidence and merely asked questions about Edward Payne's occupation and previous employers. Payne confirmed that he was a labourer by trade and worked on and off for a Mr Parfitt, whose business premises were on Westminster Bridge Road, Lambeth, South London. In addition Payne stated that he had mentioned to Millar that he believed it to be a curious place to dig a ditch and that he thought an elbow joint might be needed to let the water closet drain.

When one takes an objective look at the evidence given by the four witnesses so far, it is fair to assume that Elias Huelin and Ann Boss had already been murdered prior to Walter Millar approaching Edward Payne at the Admiral Keppel public house at 12.30 p.m. on Monday, 9 May. Therefore, when Payne entered No. 24 Wellington Square later that afternoon to dig what was to be Elias Huelin's grave, the unfortunate victim was no doubt secreted somewhere in the house. A picture was carefully being drawn for the jury, of a ruthless and evil man, a man who was so confident his crimes would never be discovered that he invited a labourer into the house, showed him around the property and got him to dig a grave before dismissing him. Of course, this invitation was a big mistake as Edward Payne's evidence was incriminatory; it was a mistake Millar would repeat a second time, two days later.

Following the compelling evidence delivered by Edward Payne, the prosecution returned the jury's attention back to events of Monday, 9 May and introduced the court to the Millars' family friend and prosecution witness, Harriett Sibley. The prosecution knew at this stage that they had no direct evidence per se that would convict Walter Millar of the murders of Huelin and Boss and no witnesses that could connect the victims to Walter Millar on Monday, 9 May. So the prosecution would have to rely heavily on the circumstantial evidence to build a picture of the events surrounding the murders, to the extent that a jury would convict. Harriett Sibley would be the first of several witnesses the prosecution would rely upon to create this image.

Harriett Sibley introduced herself to the court as a widow who lived at No. 6 Rutland Place, Knightsbridge. She stated that she had known the Millars for two years and had visited Mrs Millar on Sunday, 8 May and returned the following day, arriving about 3.30 p.m. Sibley claimed that on 9 May Walter Millar had just arrived home from work (this would have been about half an hour after Millar had left Edward Payne). Sibley said to the court that Millar was in the process of cleaning himself to have dinner and that he put on a clean shirt, freshly ironed by his wife, after finishing his meal. He then left the house, stating he was going to Hornsey in North London regarding future work. When Sibley left at 10 p.m., Millar had not returned. The judge asked Sibley about Millar's wearing of whiskers (what we would describe today as bushy sideburns; the style covered a great area of each cheek and was very fashionable during Victorian times, often described as 'mutton chops').

'How long before had you seen him [Millar] with whiskers?' Her answer, which was ambiguous, only aided the defence's case:

> I had not seen him with whiskers that I am aware of, from the time twelve months ago till Sunday night previous. I had seen him with whiskers before; I could not say how long before; I have left this house for twelve months [she had previously lodged with the family]. I had seen him casually, but I had never taken notice of his whiskers. I was there on Sunday afternoon, the 8th, to tea, I think he had whiskers then, but I could not swear to it.

Mr Beasley for the prosecution attempted to get the conversation back to a stronger position for the Crown when he asked her:

'You say you stayed until 10 o'clock on this Monday night. Did he come back before you left?'

'No.'

'Have you ever seen the defendant Walter Millar wear spectacles?'

'I have never known him to wear spectacles as a rule; I have seen him put on a pair of spectacles, for fun, in his own apartment, but I never as a rule saw him wear spectacles.'

The defence, as you would expect, reverted to the somewhat cloudy issue of Millar's whiskers, asking if Sibley was aware if Millar had ever mentioned that he sometimes shaved off his whiskers during the summer months.

'Yes, I have heard him say many times that in summer he shaved off his whiskers; I saw him do it one summer; that was the summer I lodged with him, that would be two years ago – he was always doing something to his whiskers.'

The defence then tried to refute the idea that this man was a cold-blooded, callous killer by asking Harriett Sibley about Walter Millar's demeanour when he had arrived home shortly before her arrival on Monday, 9 May, only – as the prosecution were claiming – four or so hours after murdering Elias Huelin and even less time since the slaying of Ann Boss. Harriett Sibley was adamant Millar appeared in his:

> Usual manner on this Monday, exactly the same as I have always seen him; I saw no change whatever in him; I saw nothing unusual about him, he was full of his fun, the same as he always has been – I mean he was laughing and joking the same as I have usually known him to do – his wife and child were there.

The efforts of the defence team to undermine the prosecution's case had started in earnest.

John Hunt, the Paultons Square keeper, was the next witness called. The prosecution established him to be the last person to see Ann Boss alive. His evidence was followed by that of the baker Sidney Ball who had attempted to deliver bread to the address at No. 15 Paultons Square on Monday,

9 May between 12 noon and 1 p.m. but who had received no answer.

It was with some trepidation that the next witness walked into the Old Bailey courtroom. Samuel Stainsby lived at No. 14 Paultons Square, which he rented from Huelin. He had received a large degree of criticism from both the press and individual members of the Chelsea community regarding his and the Metropolitan Police's actions, or as the media and general public perceived it, their procrastination, on the night of the 9 May. Stainsby gave evidence of finding Huelin's faithful pet dog at the front door late that evening and found, when checking over the wall of his garden, that the premises of No. 15 were insecure. He took what he believed was the right course of action by walking down to Chelsea police station on King's Road and alerting the police to the situation. He confirmed that he did tell them that Huelin and Boss were due to go to Lincolnshire; he also informed them that he found it odd that they had not notified him that they were going and that Huelin had left his beloved dog to fend for itself. He described going into the house with two police constables, gaining access over his wall and through the back door of No. 15. He explained that nobody was in the house and there was no evidence of foul play. He and the police *had* seen the dark green box, which, unbeknown to them, contained the body of Ann Boss, in the back kitchen. But there was nothing about the securely locked box to attract their attention, so they did not concern themselves with it.

The public criticism of Stainsby seemed to be unwarranted, for as soon as he had alerted the police they were lawfully in charge of the situation; as the evidence suggests, Ann Boss had, by this time, been dead up to twelve hours so he could not have done much to improve the situation.

In such a short period of time, in a relatively cool part of the house, the body would not have been giving off any particular noxious aroma associated with death, and the leakage of blood had been concealed under the box and was only exposed when the box was moved. The failing – if any failings had occurred – was the inability of the two police constables to look closer at what the facts were telling them: a partially cleaned room, insecure doors and windows, the victims' failure to alert their next-door neighbour to them going away and the adored pet left outside to fend for itself. It appears the police disregarded the evidence in front of them and were happy to accept the easy option offered by the person reporting the incident.

Stainsby, in an effort to defend himself (although we must remember that he was not on trial), explained to the court that he was not completely happy with the situation and the police's response. He felt so strongly that the following morning, having again found the dog on the doorstep, he contacted Huelin's best friend John Carter. Carter entered the property while Stainsby remained outside; what Carter observed would be described by him during his testimony. Stainsby's remaining evidence surrounded sightings of the defendant utilising a hansom cab the following night (this evidence is examined a little later in the prosecution's case) and on Wednesday seeing Henry Piper's van situated outside the address. He also stated that he saw Millar at Chelsea police station, several hours after his arrest; this presumably was some form of identification process used by the police which was not documented or introduced into the evidential chain.

Stainsby was cross-examined, mainly about his relationship with Huelin, and to summarise, claimed that he had called upon him at No. 15 on several occasions due to the landlord/tenant

relationship they shared, and he added that Huelin rarely had
any visitors. Huelin had never discussed with him that he was a
native of Jersey, but he knew that some of his family lived there.
He then contradicted his evidence by noting that Huelin did
in fact mention that he had been raised in Jersey. The defence
then asked about Rebecca Evans visiting Millar on the Tuesday
night. Stainsby recalled that he was looking through his parlour
window (which he seemed to do with regularity) and heard a
woman's voice, but he could not say who it was.

As previously discussed, the prosecution's case was going
to have to rely on circumstantial evidence as there was no
direct evidence: nobody saw the murders taking place and no
forensic science such as DNA or fingerprints (dealt with in
a later chapter) was available to assist investigators; therefore,
evidence from eye-witnesses regarding continuity of identification was paramount to proving the case. The next witness
was to provide a vital link in the evidential chain, one of such
importance that Millar must have been left calculating the
days until his execution.

William Arthur, a painter by trade, informed the court that
he lodged with the Millar family from late January 1870, right
up to the night of Walter Millar's arrest for the murder of Ann
Boss on Wednesday, 11 May. His normal place of sleep was on
a made-up bed in the kitchen. He had known the defendant for
about four years and often worked alongside him in the decorat-
ing trade. Arthur told the court that he had worked for Huelin at
No. 24 Wellington Square and had painted some interior walls,
but the last time he had been at the address was on Thursday,
28 April 1870. Walter Millar was also working at the address
that day, letting Arthur in, as he had possession of the keys to
the property. Arthur was asked about any change that he had
noticed in the presentation of Millar's facial hair. He replied:

On the Monday night of that week [9 May] he had no beard on when I saw him, he had no whiskers, they were cut off; he had a tuft on the chin and a moustache, but no whiskers. He did cut off his whiskers at times, but on Monday night I perceived they were off; I must have seen him one day in the week before, but what day I can't say; he had whiskers then.

Arthur then goes onto recall events on the evening of Monday, 9 May:

I slept in the house on the Monday night, in the kitchen; the prisoner came down into the kitchen that night, I should say near about 12.15 a.m., he remained there for about five or ten minutes, he did not take supper there, he took it upstairs into his own bed-chamber. This was when I noticed that he had no whiskers, he didn't realise that I was awake and watching him. He had a moustache and a bit of hair on his chin; he did not wear that at all times, he generally always wore whiskers, he generally wore his beard rather long in front, a full beard all round, his whiskers were shaved, leaving just a little bit on the point of the chin and a moustache. He was differently dressed from his usual weekday dress; he appeared as if he had a new pair of trousers on, a sort of grey, a grey waistcoat and a darkish coat. I said to him: 'You are a regular swell; you have made yourself look rather guyish by cutting your whiskers off'. He didn't make any remark in answer to my comments, he just looked at me as much to say he had new trousers, that was what I took it [the look] to be; that was all, he took his supper upstairs and I never saw him afterwards.

The defence's cross-examination concentrated on the clothes Arthur stated he had seen the defendant wearing on the Monday night. Arthur described Millar as wearing his 'Sunday best clothes' and that he appeared to have a 'new pair of trousers on which I had never seen before'.

Arthur's evidence also proved that Walter Millar was up and about at gone midnight on the night/early morning of 9/10 May, which was a significant observation in relation to the next witness to be called.

Number 2 Sidney Mews, just a short walk from Seymour Place, was the home of Mrs Harriett Middleton. The charwoman's evidence was heard at Westminster Police Court and at the inquests into the death of Huelin and Boss. It is important to remember that Middleton had known the defendant for about three years and had actually lodged with him and his family at Hope Cottage, Stewart's Grove, Chelsea, for nearly a year and a half. They also often worked together in the properties owned by Elias Huelin. To summarise her evidence: Middleton was woken about 12.30 a.m. on the night/early morning of the 9/10 May, looked out of the window and saw a man at her door whom she did not recognise as the defendant. She enquired as to what he wanted at such a late hour. As we know, the man claimed to be the nephew of Elias Huelin – alleged by the prosecution to be Walter Millar – and he made arrangements with Middleton to attend No. 15 Paultons Square later that morning to clean and look after the house. What is important for the prosecution is the continuity her evidence provides with that of William Arthur who had seen and described Walter Millar within the previous hour. This was strengthened again when the judge asked her to describe what the man was wearing; Middleton stated that he was wearing 'light trousers, a light waistcoat and black coat'. She claimed the man was speaking in broken English with a French accent. She did *not* at any time recognise this man to be Walter Millar. Again, one must question Walter Millar's motive in employing another person who knew him well to work at the location (No. 15 Paultons

Square) where he had allegedly murdered and stored the body of his victim, just as he had done with Edward Payne in Wellington Square. Was it an excess of self-confidence that his plan couldn't fail or just a case of plain stupidity? Or perhaps it was deliberate – the danger of being caught adding to the thrill of the crime.

As we know, Mrs Harriett Middleton and her daughter went to No. 15 Paultons Square early on Tuesday, 10 May. The next significant piece of evidence she offers is the visit of Walter Millar, as himself, to her address about 8 a.m. on Tuesday morning. Presumably she again answered from the upstairs bedroom, as she states that she did not take any notice of Millar's appearance from her vantage point. Millar asked her if she had the key to No. 15 Paultons Square – on the one hand a clever ploy on Millar's part to distance himself from the person who had visited Middleton that night, but also an active admittance that he knew Middleton was in possession of the key to the property. Millar was then informed by Middleton that she did have the key (as he would have already been aware) and that she and her daughter were leaving shortly to go to Paultons Square. Millar stated that he had to: 'Go to No. 15 for my pails. I am going home to breakfast first and I will see you there.'

The Middletons went to No. 15 Paultons Square and shortly after their arrival, Walter Millar turned up. Mrs Harriett Middleton answered the door; Millar stood in front of her, his face hidden under a wrapper.

'What is the matter?' she asked.

He claimed that he had got a very bad sore throat. Middleton noticed that the wrapper covered all his face up to the top part of his ears. He reiterated that Huelin and Boss had gone to the countryside and that the house was empty.

He went into the address and collected his pails and left. The next occasion she allegedly saw Millar was that evening when he came to her house in Sidney Mews disguised as the French nephew of Elias Huelin and enquired as to why No. 15 had been left unoccupied. Mrs Harriett Middleton recognised the man from the previous night who had given her the key for No. 15 Paultons Square. He was dressed in the same clothes and again spoke in broken English with a French accent. She returned to Paultons Square with the Frenchman.

Middleton went on to recall the visit from Rebecca Evans, the confusion over Miss Evans's address and the cab journeys taken by Walter Millar (in disguise) to and from Park Walk. She also gave evidence on Elizabeth Green, the woman brought back to Paultons Square on Wednesday, 11 May, the night that the body of Ann Boss was discovered. She went on to describe the events involving the removal man Henry Piper, and the discovery of blood and eventually the body of the unfortunate housekeeper. Middleton formally identified Boss, on the basis that she had previously known her.

The cross-examination that followed was lengthy; the defence attempted to discredit Middleton's account of the events:

'What age is your daughter?'

'Eighteen last April.'

'Did she see the man who appeared on your front door on Monday night?'

'She did not see the man, she was in bed.'

Middleton was asked to give some background about how long she had known the defendant and under what circumstances. She replied:

I think it is two and a half or three years ago that I lived at the prisoner's house. I lived with him and his wife for sixteen months, we only had one room. I think I worked with the prisoner at 24, Wellington Square six days the first week and four days the latter part of the time; that was at the end of April and the beginning of May.

She was asked when she was last at the prisoner's house.

The last time I was at the prisoner's house in Seymour Place was on Sunday night, as he came to me on the Monday. I don't think I stayed more than half an hour and I got home about 9 o'clock. I don't think my place is half a mile from his, it is not half a mile from Wellington Square, I can go to it in ten minutes and from Paultons Square in a quarter of an hour.

The defence then really turned the screw in an attempt to discredit Middleton's identification evidence, referring constantly to her account of the events given at the coroner's inquest. They were successful, to some degree, in causing confusion within her own mind, which is evident in the following account. To avoid additional text the questions asked do not feature, but from the answers given one can easily follow the defence's line of questioning.

I was examined before the coroner – I don't recollect laying [stating] there, that I knew the difference between Millar and the prisoner; I did say 'Mr Millar is a Scotchman and the prisoner is a Frenchman' – that was before I knew the prisoner. I don't recollect saying that Millar was about thirty years of age, and the man charged was about forty; I can't recollect anything of the sort. I went to the police station, I might have said that Millar was not the man who I had called the Frenchman, but I did not know it was Millar, he came to me in such a disguise.

Middleton went on to say that she had never 'heard the prisoner [when in the persona of Walter Millar] speak French in the three years I have known him'.

Mr Poland, for the prosecution, attempted to mend some of the damage created by the cross-examination of his agitated and unreliable witness:

'Are you quite sure that the man who was downstairs with Piper when the box was corded, was the man that had called on you on the Monday night and went over to the house with you and looked into the bureau on the Tuesday night?'

'Yes.'

'Did he have spectacles on?'

'Yes, he wore spectacles all the time, I can't say whether they were light or dark, my sight is not very good.'

Lord Chief Justice Cockburn could see the obvious importance of getting the spectacles issue to the forefront of the jury's minds. 'Had he spectacles on, on the Monday night?' he asked the witness.

'Yes,' she replied, 'and on Tuesday and on Wednesday, and when they corded the box he had them on. I never knew him wear spectacles when I knew him as Millar, the working man.' She reiterated the same point when asked by the judge about the French accent:

> The man who came on Monday night spoke broken English, so did he on Tuesday and on Wednesday, when Piper was there. On Monday he was dressed in light trousers, a light waistcoat and black coat, and the same on Tuesday. I can't say as to the Wednesday night, for I did not notice, there was such bother with the box and all that, I never noticed.

It would seem that with the judge's guidance, Mrs Harriett Middleton had finished her evidence with the conviction and confidence that had at first deserted her. Would her daughter corroborate her mother's evidence or was it about to go very wrong for the Crown?

Miss Harriett Middleton was mature beyond her years, speaking with confidence. She corroborated her mother's evidence and remembered other important points which had so far been overlooked. She told the jury of two saucepans on the fire that had gone out, one filled with a partially cooked pudding and the other with water ready for the prepared vegetables that lay nearby. Her thoughts of somebody abandoning the house in a hurry were enforced when she arrived at the first floor of the house and found that the floor had been partly cleaned. On the floor lay a coarse cleaning apron, three cloths, a pail of water, a scrubbing brush, soap and a flannel. Miss Middleton told the court that it looked like 'somebody had been scrubbing and then thrown the apron down in a hurry and left'.

She also remembered Walter Millar arriving at the house in his work clothes with the wrap around his face, going out into the back garden to retrieve his pail and a brush before his departure from the house. Miss Middleton recalled two visitors to the house that day: John Carter, a close friend of Elias Huelin, and Eliza Bartlett, the maid of Rebecca Evans, who had brought a key to another property and left it there. Harriett described her return home and the arrival of the Frenchman later that evening. She noted that he had no whiskers, but that he did have a dark moustache and was wearing spectacles. She added that he was aggressive and had been drinking. Due to his drunken state, her mother refused her permission to return to the house with him, so she returned to No. 15 Paultons Square herself. She added that she assumed he was a Frenchman or a foreigner at the time. Yet after his arrest, she saw him in custody and did think he had a likeness to Walter Millar, but the disguise was so convincing she still believed him to be a Frenchman.

Miss Harriett Middleton's cross-examination was as thorough as her mother's, but the young girl seemed prepared and delivered her answers with apparent honesty and integrity.

'Were you examined before the coroner?' was the first question.

'Yes, and also before the magistrate.' She then went on to answer several questions about the occasions she had seen the defendant either as Walter Millar himself or allegedly as the disguised Frenchman:

> I said it was not the prisoner who came on the Monday night, but a Frenchman – I did not see him that night [Monday 9 May], I heard him – I have also said previously that I saw that person again, he came on Tuesday night to mother's – I did not see him [the Frenchman] during the day on Tuesday, it was in the evening, dark between 8 and 9 o'clock. I knew Millar before, when mother lived there [as a lodger] and I went three or four times to Wellington Square, when he and mother were working there.

Lord Chief Justice Cockburn asked, 'Did you observe how the man was dressed on the Tuesday night?

'Yes, he had a high hat on, spectacles, a black coat and light trousers; I say he was a Frenchman because he looked tall and looked very much like French; everything in his way, as he stood, made me think he was a Frenchman – I can't point out any peculiarity, only that.'

The next three witnesses were Rebecca Evans, the former tenant of Elias Huelin, her maid Eliza Bartlett and Thomas Herbert, the hansom cab driver who was hired by the Frenchman to take him to Park Walk. They all repeated the evidence they had given previously in the police court, with no particular revelations coming to light during cross- or re-examination of their evidence. Herbert did inform the court during his cross-examination that he had been taken by the police to Newgate Prison, where he recognised Millar as the man in his cab.

The butcher, William Pilditch, was the next to give his account. He recalled being approached by the disguised prisoner on the morning of Tuesday, 10 May at about 11.15, enquiring about the availability of property to let on Dieppe Street, North End, Fulham. He gave his account as stated in the police court and was asked during cross-examination:

'How was he dressed when you saw him?'

> In a light loose suit, not exactly a working suit such as you would see a working man with on an evening; not like a gentleman, nor exactly as a working-man; like a working-man when off work and going out for two or three hours. He did not give me any name or address. I am sure the prisoner is the man – he said he was going to teach two or three languages. When he first spoke to me I thought he was a Scotchman from his accent; when he came again I did not know what he was, whether he was English, Irish, Scotch, or French; sometimes he would talk like a Frenchman, something I could not understand.

Elizabeth Green, the female companion picked up by the defendant on 11 May in the Haymarket area of central London, was next to give evidence. She explained the circumstances around their meeting and admitted that after the defendent had wined and dined her, that she was extremely drunk and that he took her shopping for a new outfit of clothes. She was aware that she had been transported to a house somewhere in Chelsea, where another woman was present (Mrs Harriett Middleton), and that she had another drink before refusing a second. Green denied ever seeing a box in the kitchen or the van driver (Henry Piper), stating that the wine had probably overcome her and that she had no recollection of what took place in the house or how she got away. Green then confirmed that later that morning she was arrested for being drunk but could not remember where she was detained; only that she appeared in front of a magistrate soon after. Her evidence was inconclusive, as was her identification of the suspect, stating that, 'I pointed out two or three men as the person at first.'

The witnesses called so far by the prosecution had been a mixed bunch. The value of those such as Edward Payne and William Arthur had laid a sound foundation for the prosecution's case, while the defence had muddied the waters with an effective cross-examination of Mrs Harriett Middleton, especially around the question of identification. It only takes a seed of doubt to form in the minds of a few jury members for the defendant to walk out of court an innocent man in the eyes of the law.

The prosecution still had not categorically proved to the jury that the Frenchman, who stated he was the nephew of Elias Huelin, was one and the same as Walter Millar. Could the next witness provide this critical piece of evidence? The tension in the court was palpable; heads turned and bobbed in order to get first sight of Henry Piper as he confidently entered the witness box and with a clear voice took the oath and gave his name and address.

Piper's evidence at the police court had been widely reported in many newspapers, and a low hum of whispering gathered pace as the court waited for prosecution counsel Mr Poland to begin his examination. The disturbance was quelled and the court returned to order under the belligerent stare of Lord Chief Justice Cockburn and his utterance of the words 'contempt of court'. In a case that lacked hard evidence

Piper's account was paramount to the prosecution's case, his evidence so crucial it is worthy of re-examination:

> I am a van proprietor and greengrocer and live in Marlborough Road, Chelsea. On Wednesday night, 11 May, the prisoner called on me about 9.20. The shop was shut; he summoned me to the door and said 'did I have a machine or a cart?' He talked it in quite a French accent; I thought he was a Frenchman. I asked him what it was to do, he replied, 'To remove some luggage'.

Piper had asked several more questions regarding the location, time and price of the job, pointing out the fact that it was late at night, the distance he would have to travel and that it was raining heavily outside. The prisoner replied, 'in half an hour's time' and 'me pay you anything you charge, you make your charge and I will pay'. In relation to the destination of the luggage he replied 'to Fulham, the West End'. Piper noted that the man had seemed very agitated and that he had watched him return to a cab which was situated some distance away.

Piper had prepared his van and travelled the three-quarters of a mile from his address near Sloane Square, in the company of an employee called George, to No. 15 Paultons Square. On his arrival, he knocked on the door, which was opened by Mrs Middleton who invited him in. Piper saw the prisoner come out of the dining room and was told that some of the luggage was upstairs and some downstairs. They had all gone down and the prisoner put his hand into the front parlour and retrieved a bundle of rope. Piper takes up the story:

> The box stood in the back kitchen, under the wall, on the left-hand side. The prisoner said, 'I want that box corded.' I pointed out that it didn't need cording as it would stand in the bottom of the van. He stated that

he wanted the box cording and that he would do the cording himself. He went about it the wrong way and I took the cord out of his hand and made the loop at the end and put it under the box. After I had got the rope round over the lock and under the box I picked the other end of the box up, with my left hand, on its end, to make a half hitch with the rope underneath, and I felt something was on my hand. I looked at it by candle-light and saw it was blood. The prisoner stood on my right and Mrs Middleton on my left. I said to him 'what does this mean?' I then got the box out about 2ft from the wall and looking on the floor I saw that there was a pool of blood, where I had lifted the box from. I asked the man a second time what it meant but he never answered me. I asked Mrs Middleton if she knew what was in the box, as there was something not quite right. The prisoner was wearing a light coat at the time, buttoned by the top button. He did not stop to unbutton it, but wrenched it off over his head and threw it down into the blood and then stamped upon it. All this time I had got the box up on its end, resting on my hip.

At this point Piper mentioned the presence of Elizabeth Green who was standing at the foot of the stairs leading from the kitchen to the upper levels of the house. Piper continued:

I told the prisoner that I should not remove the box until he showed me what was inside it. At this point I saw Elizabeth Green run upstairs and the prisoner followed her, and I followed him. He stopped on the middle of the stairs and said to me, 'Go back and cord that box.' I said 'not me'; he stamped his foot on the stairs and said, 'Go back carman and cord the box and do your work.'

It was then that Piper realised that the prisoner had lost his accent.

It was the first time I noticed him not talk like a Frenchman; he talked like an Englishman as I am talking to you now. I again repeated that

'I shall not, I don't mean losing you, I don't mean to lose sight of you.'
He walked out into Paultons Square and turned to the left towards
the King's Road.

The prisoner had picked up his coat from the floor of the kitchen before following Green upstairs and, as he headed toward King's Road, he put it back on. Piper followed at a short distance, crucially for the prosecution case never losing sight of the prisoner. He went on to describe to the court his meeting with PC Coles and their actions thereafter.

Henry Piper was a very concerned man; he had already gone beyond the duty of a responsible citizen and his instincts were telling him that something horrendous had happened in No. 15 and that the man impersonating a Frenchman was deeply involved. He would have felt more comfortable, he said, if the police constable had taken hold of the Frenchman. However, the officer appeared inexperienced and unsure of his powers in this situation; it would probably have been the first time in his career that he faced such a serious dilemma. Did he arrest the suspect on the say-so of the accuser and on what evidence? After all, the man was only surmising that the substance on his hand was in fact human blood: no victim had yet been found and the suspect was walking back to the possible scene of the crime unaided and willingly.

The next pieces in this puzzle follow the same sequence as in previous accounts; they arrived at the address, Piper asked George to run to the police station and inform them of what had happened and who had sent him. It was at this point that the man became quite unnerved and fidgety. Piper told Coles to attempt to hold the prisoner down. Piper recalled what happened next:

We were walking to and fro, when we were walking towards the King's Road, the prisoner in the middle, I on the kerb and the constable next to the houses; all at once the prisoner took a spring and away he went. I shouted 'There, now he has gone!' He was running at the height of his speed, he knocked off his hat into the road and then pulled off his coat and threw that in the road. I followed him at the height of my speed, calling out after him 'Stop Thief!' and 'Murder' as loud as I could. He ran the best part of half a mile; the constable was some way behind me. We came to a very narrow part, where the people hearing the cry of 'Murder' were standing close under the shop windows, and that left little room for the prisoner to run, he had to take to the kerb.

Piper was exasperated at the non-action of the bystanders, but this made him even more determined to catch his man. As it became apparent that the man might escape, Piper was at last blessed with some luck as his quarry slipped off the kerb and fell on his face.

I was within ten yards of him and before he had time to get up I was upon him and collared him. The policeman came up, and I asked if he would lay hold of him then, he said 'yes' we then both took him back through Paultons Square towards King's Road and there I met more assistance coming down that I had sent for. I saw Sergeant Large and two or three privates and I gave him in (to their) charge.

Sergeant Large, from whom we shall hear later, instructed PC Coles and the other officers to take the prisoner to Chelsea police station.

Piper then explained to Sergeant Large what had taken place from his arrival at No. 15 Paultons Square, up until the chase and arrest of the suspect. Both Piper and Large entered the property and Piper pointed out the box which he had moved, which led to the discovery of the blood on the floor. The sergeant acted decisively as there may have been somebody still alive inside. He got the kitchen poker and wrenched the box lid open. Piper described the disturbing scene presented to him:

> It contained the body of a woman all doubled up; she was dressed apparently as if she had just left work. A doctor was called for. I saw the rope tied round her neck, a similar bit to that which the prisoner got out of the kitchen to cord the box with; it was a piece of clothes line.

Peculiarly, there seems to be no record of any defence cross-examination. Reports in the media described a shocked silence as Piper stood down from the witness box; it was the first time during the trial that an eye-witness had described the barbaric truth of events that had taken place at No. 15 Paultons Square. All those present in the courtroom must have visualised the suffering endured by the housekeeper, who had at one moment been preparing a meal in the kitchen or scrubbing the floor, and the next had her life snuffed out as a result of a ferocious act of violence. The only person who allegedly knew what had happened in the house and how Ann Boss met her end was sitting in the dock. What could never be disputed was the terror she must have felt in the final few moments of her life.

Henry Piper was called back into the witness box some time later, and it would be prudent to deal with those issues now. The defence had a final attempt to discredit the identification evidence. Piper had linked many unanswered questions together during his testimony. Crucially, he proved that Walter Millar and the Frenchman were one and the same.

'The coat which the prisoner took off,' explained Henry Piper, 'and threw on the blood was a light coat, a little lighter than the trousers he was wearing. I can't say positively what became of the coat; he picked it up again, I think, when I told him I would not move the box, and followed the woman, Green, upstairs.'

The questions then turned to the vital identification evidence: 'I did not stay down [stairs] a minute, I followed him immediately.' Piper was adamant about this: he was a clever man and would have been prepared for the obvious accusations, however implausible, that the man arrested by him and PC Coles was not the man who had been present in the kitchen of No. 15 Paultons Square and subsequently not the man standing in the dock. He continued:

> He was only three stairs above me and the woman in front of him, she continued out and he stopped on the stairs and had a little conversation with me; he did not go out into the street without me at all. I was not a quarter of a yard from the time he came out of the kitchen until he took the spring away from me and then he was not more than ten yards from me – I kept him in sight all the time.

The court was adjourned for the day and the jury were taken to a hotel overnight, so they would not be influenced by family, friends or any media coverage that would undoubtedly feature in the next morning's press.

12

THE TRIAL: DAY TWO

THURSDAY, 14 JULY 1870

The morning newspapers flew off the stands as people were eager to read the in-depth account of the highest-profile criminal case of 1870. The crowds blocked all road approaches to the Old Bailey, keen to get a glimpse of the defendant, his family and the witnesses, who had almost become celebrities over the last couple of months.

Police Sergeant John Large was the first witness of the morning session; he corroborated much of Piper's evidence with his own account:

> I went downstairs with him and he showed me a green box, but it was locked and had this piece of cord [produced by Large as an exhibit in the court and shown to the judge and jury] put round it once. I moved the box and saw a quantity of blood on the spot that I had moved it from. I then took a poker from the fireplace and broke the box open and in it I found the body of a female.

It was at this stage that Mrs Harriett Middleton looked into the box and identified the deceased female as the housekeeper, Ann Boss. Large continued:

> I found that she was cold and I sent for a doctor. Doctor Ryder arrived in a few minutes and on moving the body I found this piece of cord round her neck. After taking it off the neck I put it together with the other cord that was round the box and found that it corresponded, it appeared to have been cut, it was the same cord. I took it off the neck; it was tied very tightly and the knot was just under the ear sufficiently tight to cause strangulation. The blood came from the mouth and nose of the female; it had run down the side of the box.

The prosecution counsel Mr Poland asked Large to describe the box to the court.

'The box was 2ft 11in long, 1ft 6in wide and 1ft 7in deep; it was an old box painted green, a wooden one with no covering to it. I, afterwards, searched the place upstairs and found a quantity of bedding tied up, ready to be removed.'

This corroborates the evidence of Henry Piper, who recalled the prisoner stating he had luggage both upstairs and down to be moved.

Sergeant Large then crucially provided the jury with direct evidence linking Walter Millar to the box in which the dead woman, Ann Boss, had been found:

> I then went to the station and asked the inspector on duty [Inspector Pitt Tarlton] whether any key was found on the prisoner. The prisoner was lying down in the room, I don't know whether he understood or not. I received a bunch of keys from Inspector Tarlton and I went back to the house and found that one of the keys fitted the lock on the box.

Large produced the key for examination by the jury, but there is no record that he produced the lock from the box. Cross-examination was initiated with a closed question: 'You forced open the box, you say?'

'Yes,' Sergeant Large replied, anticipating the next question, 'with a poker, I forced the lid right off.'

He was asked again about the key which he had produced in court.

'I took this [indicating the key] off in the presence of the inspector and returned him the others.'

Questioned about the luggage he had found upstairs he answered, 'The things that were packed ready to be removed were a bed, blankets, pillows and a bolster; they were in a room upstairs.'

The inexperienced Police Constable Joseph Coles was next in the witness box. Having introduced himself to the court and taken the oath, he informed the court that he had been in the Metropolitan Police for just two years. He recalled the night of 11 May and his meeting with Henry Piper. He corroborates a great deal of Piper's evidence, but two accounts are never going to tally exactly and it is worth examining certain differences, just as the defence and the jury would do, in the police constable's recollection. We take up his evidence at the point where Henry Piper has told PC Coles the circumstances of his employment and his discovery of blood on his hands and under the box: '… when he was moving it (the box) he got his hand all over in blood and he believed there was something wrong, he wished me to go down and see what the matter was. As soon as Piper said there was something wrong the prisoner repeated "something wrong, something wrong" about three times.'

It was at this stage that PC Coles gives his slightly different recollection of events:

When I got to 15 Paultons Square with the prisoner, I wanted to go inside the house; all three of us to go in together, to see what were the matter. He [the prisoner] would not go in, he did not say a word but he turned around from the door as though he would rather go back, he did not go in. I said to Piper, 'We had better get someone else and see what the matter is.' Piper sent off his man to the police station for another constable. After the man had been gone about three minutes the prisoner became restless and began to walk backwards and forwards past the door, and when in the direction of Danvers Street leading to the waterside, he suddenly made a bolt and ran about 400 yards. He went to step off the kerb and tripped up. I ran after him, Piper got to him first a few yards before me, about twenty yards. I then said to Piper, 'We will take him now, I don't want anything else, I know he has done something wrong or he would not run away' and I took him to the police station.

Coles, on the instruction of Sergeant Large, took the prisoner to Chelsea police station and searched him. All the property found on the prisoner (already listed in a previous chapter) was handed over and listed by the duty inspector, Pitt Tarlton.

During his cross-examination Coles explained that he and Piper had walked up and down Paultons Square with the prisoner 'for about three minutes after Piper's man had gone for another constable, I was not with him more than seven or eight minutes before the prisoner ran away. Piper did not tell me to take him in charge or to lay hold of him; he whispered in my ear and said he thought he meant to bolt.' Questions arose about the continuity of the property taken from the prisoner, especially concerning the all-important bunch of keys.

Coles produced a list on a piece of paper: 'This paper I have is the list of the property I took from the prisoner, Inspector Tarlton made it out after I had taken the property from him.

I don't think the keys were included in that list but I remember taking the keys from him perfectly well.'

This revelation of an inconsistency with the continuity of the exhibit could break open the prosecution's case and would definitely have caused a few gasps in the courtroom. This could lead to all sorts of allegations, such as the police planting the keys on the defendant after they found them in the house and attributing them to the defendant to prove his guilt, or that the keys were found on the body of the deceased, Ann Boss, and then attributed to the prisoner. This was indeed bad news for the prosecution and they would soon have to attempt damage control.

Coles continued, 'I have added the (broken) bottle in pencil. I found that in his left hand trouser pocket, smashed; I did not drop and break it, I took it out of his pocket all in small pieces, it seemed a small bottle, I could not say the size of it because it was all smashed up.' Coles was later recalled to produce a coat and pair of boots, 'the coat is the one that the prisoner threw off and I also produce the one he had on underneath; these boots he had on when he was taken.'

The damage control came in the form of the duty inspector for the Chelsea Police District on the night of 11 May, Pitt Tarlton, the next witness to give evidence:

When the prisoner was brought in I saw him searched and the constable gave the things into my possession. I have heard the evidence given today as to the things he [PC Coles] found, this is the correct list of them, but the keys are not mentioned in the list. I directed the sergeant to make two lists and the keys were omitted in each, I put the keys down on my own list [up to three lists now], the keys were found and handed to me and the following morning I entered the property found on the charge sheet and afterwards the sergeant made a list from the charge sheet [4th list]. I am certain the keys were found at that time; I gave this one key [producing the key to the court] to the witness Large.

Tarlton then went on to give account of the episode with the broken bottle and the physical state of the prisoner, but this will be dealt with in more detail when we examine the evidence of Dr Godrich.

Tarlton also describes the charging of Water Millar with the murders of Elias Huelin and Ann Boss and his replies to these charges. As one would imagine, the cross-examination concentrated on the apparent procedural error in not listing the keys allegedly found on the defendant:

'Where were all the things put to that were taken from the prisoner's person?' the defence asked.

'Tied up in this handkerchief and placed in my desk at the station,' replied Tarlton, before continuing:

Neither of these lists is my writing, they are the reserve sergeant's. I gave the list to him or read it out and he entered the things [on to the charge sheet], he left out the keys. This [the charge sheet produced to the court] was not made the same night that the things were found. All the things were rolled up in this handkerchief except the bottle; that was sealed up in a larger bottle and given to Mr Godrich.

The media at the time had tried to insinuate that Walter Millar had attempted to kill himself by ingesting a quantity of laudanum, a common drug widely used within Victorian society. Opium and its derivative laudanum were the 'celebrity' drugs of Victorian England but were also widely used as painkillers. Samuel Taylor Coleridge, Thomas De Quincey, Wilkie Collins and Charles Dickens were all known users of laudanum. Fictional characters also often relied on the drug such as Conan Doyle's Sherlock Holmes and Mary Shelley's Victor Frankenstein. Laudanum was widely available and contained about 10 per cent opium and 90 per cent water flavoured with either cinnamon or saffron. From the evidence provided by Henry Piper and PC Coles, it was unlikely Walter Millar ever consumed any quantity of laudanum in an effort to kill himself. Yet it is clear that he was in possession of the drug and may have been under its influence prior to his arrest. The facts reveal that while he was under the watch of Piper, he never had a chance to drink any of the drug and soon after that he escaped from the scene of one of his crimes, fell and, in the process, broke the bottle in his pocket. Dr Godrich seems to agree that any attempted suicide bid was pure dramatisation:

I saw the prisoner there, lying on the floor, I spoke to him in English and in French as the police said they were informed that he was a Frenchman, he did not answer at all. I examined him, he was in a very depressed state, weak and pale and either could not or would not move his limbs. The police showed me a broken bottle and some small pieces wrapped up in a piece of paper; there was a torn label on it which read 'Laudanum'. I fancy it smelt of laudanum. Thinking that he might have taken laudanum I gave him an emetic with coffee and brandy which he drank freely without difficulty; the emetic acted, I examined the result; there were no traces of poison whatsoever; if laudanum had been recently taken it must have been found. I thought he was shimming insensibility for his pupils acted naturally and his pulse was regular though weak. I stayed a considerable time and saw him twice next morning. I analysed the bottle and found distinct traces of opium or laudanum.

During his cross-examination, Dr Godrich accepted that opium was used for the relief of toothache and all sorts of other painful conditions. He also agreed that the defendant may have had as much as two glasses of brandy, or more, given to him on his instructions on the account of his depressed state. He gave directions to the police that he should have a little more if necessary. He denied that he propped Millar's mouth open with a piece of wood, yet confirmed that he did attempt to introduce the stomach pump. However, Millar clenched his teeth together and broke the mouthpiece, so he was unable to administer it.

So far, the trial had concentrated on the movement, behaviour and arrest of the defendant Walter Millar, as well as the discovery of the body of Ann Boss. The evidence was mounting: the testimonies (in particular those of Edward Payne, William Arthur and Henry Piper); the compelling evidence found on the person of the prisoner Walter Millar, which included the title deeds of No. 24 Wellington Square, the envelopes addressed to Ann Boss and the key which fitted the lock on the box in which the deceased was found. The gruesome unearthing of Elias Huelin had not yet been mentioned, but that was about to change as the prosecution's case moved from Paultons Square to Wellington Square, half a mile away.

As we will discuss in a later chapter, crime scene management was very much in its infancy. The crime scene was protected by police from the public, but that was more of a necessity to allow the police to uncover the truth about what happened without interference rather than preserving the scene to protect vital forensic evidence; methods of detection such as the analysis of fingerprints, traces of blood or DNA did not yet exist.

On Thursday, 12 May 1870, detective officers Edward Clough and William Watts had been instructed to meet Superintendent Fisher, the officer in charge of the case, at No. 24 Wellington Square in order to begin a search of the house in an attempt to discover the whereabouts of Elias Huelin, who at that time, of course, was merely missing. On entering the property and proceeding to the back kitchen, the clues began to form a picture of what happened to the missing man. Detective Officer Edward Clough guided the court through what he saw:

> In the back kitchen I found this pick and shovel [produced to the court by the officer, belonging, as we now know, to Edward Payne] and under the boards by the sink I found this hat [which he also produced] all battered in as it is now, it lay between the rafters, crushed; no doubt it had been pressed there, the lining was wet with blood. We began digging in the back yard and knocked off at 8.30 that evening; there was a quantity of clotted blood and paper lying in the yard but we did not find a body; the paper looked as if it had been torn off the walls. The paper and the blood were all mixed up together. I noticed that there had been a new flooring board laid in the back kitchen about 1½ft or 2ft from the back window.

The search continued the following day, Friday, 13 May, and as we have already heard, the breakthrough came from the evidence of Edward Payne, who pointed out to Fisher, Clough and Watts exactly where he had dug a drain hole at the directions of the defendant. The court was in complete silence, the tension thicker than the London smog – every person present knew what was coming.

Clough described the horrific scene:

I went to the house again on Friday, between 1 and 2 o'clock in the afternoon, the witness Payne was there and he pointed out where he had dug the drain. I and Watts dug up the earth there and found the body of the Reverend Huelin. Watts found the upper part of the body, I found the legs lying near the wall. He had on his shirt, gloves, mittens, trousers, boots and cravat but no coat or hat. I found the coat after we removed the body and placed it in the backroom. It [the coat] was underneath where the body lay, below the head a foot below the surface of the gravel; one sleeve of the coat was turned inside out. I afterwards noticed the neck of the deceased, there was a piece of rope tied tightly round the neck. I saw Watts cut it [the rope] off. I sent for Mr Turner the surgeon to examine the body. I afterwards examined the floor in the front kitchen and saw the marks of, apparently, a red substance, I can't say whether it was blood or not, the marks appeared to have been scrubbed.

Detective William Watts supported the evidence given by his fellow officer, corroborating the fact that he saw that blood-stained hat, that he assisted in the discovery of the corpse and that he removed the rope from the deceased's neck, which had been tied tightly with the knot under the right ear. He produced the length of rope to the court stating that it was 11in long.

The defence seemed to accept the fact that the evidence given by both detectives was factual and correct as there appears to be no record of any cross-examination. However, Lord Chief Justice Cockburn wanted to know about the storage of the body.

'Did you find any traces of blood indicating where the body had been deposited between death and the putting it in the drain?'

'There were stains of blood on the floor in the kitchen,' replied Watts, 'and I believe some were found in a closet, but not by me. I saw the stains in the front kitchen, they appeared to me to be stains of blood; some strong chemicals had been used with a view of getting them out, so as to turn them white. And in the direction of the back place where the body was found, there were two or three spots, I believe of blood, which had been cleaned.'

The surgeon who attended No. 24 Wellington Square, Thomas Aubrey Turner, was next to give his account. He informed the court what he had found on his arrival at the scene, his initial observations around the cause of death and his subsequent post-mortem examination, with his opinion as to the most likely weapon used and the conclusion that Huelin had died from the force of blows to his head. He also commented that he had examined the house and found, in the cupboard under the basement stairs, several spots of blood on the wall, about half a yard from the ground, which appeared to have dripped from a wound. He was shown the stain on the floor that had been partially scrubbed, as described by Clough and Watts. The prosecution, probably anticipating questions from the judge, asked the surgeon:

'Supposing a body had been placed in that cupboard after the wounds behind the ear had been inflicted, leaning against the wall, would blood have come from that?'

'It is probable; the cupboard was not long enough for the body to lay out straight, it might have been partially doubled up. The cupboard door was open when I saw it; it had been opened for me to see.'

'Did you attend Mr Huelin professionally?'

'No, but I knew him very well.'

Other questions were asked to which his replies were:

I did not know for certain that he had any acquaintances in Jersey or France. I had heard about the neighbourhood that he had, he never told me that he was a native of Jersey. I had only known him for about two years; he was a heavy, stout man, I should think he was over 11 stone, nearly 12. I did not see the clotted blood in the yard of which the officers have spoken. I did not see any blood upon the walls, except in the cupboard. I did not examine the house thoroughly; they [the police] showed me, casually, the parts that had been rubbed out.

The prosecution case was now nearing its end; the last police witness was Inspector James Pay from the detective branch at Scotland Yard. He recalled his role in the investigation from visiting the defendant's wife, accompanying her to Chelsea police station where she positively identified the mysterious Frenchman as her husband. He also gave evidence of finding the bloodstained working trousers identified by Mrs Millar as belonging to her husband. Inspector Pay aided the court to understand the topography of the area and the physical distances involved between several of the significant locations:

I have walked and measured the distances of the different places that have been mentioned. From 24 Wellington Square to 15 Paultons Square is 1,222 yards and it took ten minutes to walk, walking at a moderate pace. From 15 Paultons Square to the Admiral Keppel public house in the Brompton Road is 1,463 yards, walked in fourteen minutes. From the Admiral Keppel to 24 Wellington Square is 1,151 yards, time walking eleven minutes. From Mrs Middleton's house to Paultons Square is 918 yards, walked in about eight minutes; and from Wellington Square to 26 Seymour Place, the prisoner's house is 1,999 yards, that took about twenty minutes. From the Hand and Flower public house at Sands End, Fulham, to Mr Pilditch's at North End is 1,790- yards, twenty minutes' walk.

Up until that point, the judge and jury had known the victims only as names on an indictment. Elias Huelin's nephew Edward would change that, his perspective revealing a human side to the victims and showing the true tragedy of the crimes and how the murders had affected the families. He would also provide some very good evidence for the prosecution which would contribute, he hoped, to the proving of the case, the execution of the murderer and justice for his uncle. The prosecution carefully led the young Edward through the most tragic of circumstances; what follows is a summary of his evidence:

> I am the nephew of the deceased; his name was Elias Huelin, he was a clergyman and would have been 84 years of age on 19 June last. In May last I was living in Lincolnshire; my uncle had a farm there, he went down there generally about once a year. I was expecting him every day about this time. I used to live with him at 15 Paultons Square until 24 March last. He lived there alone with only Ann Boss as his housekeeper, no other servant. He had property in the neighbourhood, Nos 15, 24 and 32 Paultons Square belonged to him. I came up to London upon hearing of the murder on Thursday 12 May; the police came down to make inquiries of me and I came up the following day. I saw the body of my uncle.

A number of exhibits discovered during the investigation were produced to the court and shown to Edward Huelin.

'I have seen the different things that have been produced,' he commented and continued:

> I know this rent book [most of the items produced to him were found on the person of Walter Millar following his arrest], it is all in my handwriting, except the first page, that is in my uncle's handwriting;

it was written sometime at the beginning of last year. I know this abstract of title with the blood on it. 'No. 24 Wellington Square' is my uncle's writing. I don't know the writing on these envelopes addressed 'Ann Boss'. These spectacles belonged to my uncle and this pencil case was his. I have been shown a green box by the police; it was the box of Ann Boss, she used to keep her clothes in it.

Edward Huelin also went on to identify the boots and dark coat worn by Walter Millar at the time of his arrest as property belonging to his late uncle.

During his cross-examination Edward was questioned about the last time he had seen his uncle, and replied 'on 24 March'. He was also asked about his deceased uncle's antecedents. He stated to the court that his uncle 'was a native of Jersey, he had relations there, two nephews and three nieces and maybe cousins, and he was on good terms with them all'.

'Were you his favourite nephew?' asked the defence.

'I don't know that I was the favourite nephew; perhaps I may come in to the bulk of his property, I believe he left a will.' From the very little information known about Walter Millar's defence, some media reports suggest that Millar said he did not commit the murders and hinted that one of Elias Huelin's nephews was in fact involved. This accusation from Millar seems to be supported by the line of questioning now adopted by the defence:

'Is it true that you are likely to receive four-fifths of your uncle's estate?'

'I don't know about four-fifths of the property,' exclaimed Edward Huelin, 'I have the property in Lincolnshire and the rest of the property, with the exception of several leasehold houses. Mr Wright, my solicitor, is in court.'

Lord Chief Justice Cockburn asked, 'Do you know the relations in Jersey?'

'Yes,' replied Edward Huelin, 'they could not speak English very well, not quite as well as I do, I should think. I have been five years in England.'

Elias Huelin's closest confidant John Carter was then called:

'I knew the Reverend Mr Huelin twenty-five years; I knew also his housekeeper, Ann Boss, very well.'

He was shown the articles of clothing and asked if he could identify them.

'I recognise these boots and spectacles to be Mr Huelin's, and this hat I have brushed many times.' He continued with his account in answer to questions:

I saw him on the Sunday morning before his death, it would be about 8 o'clock I think; he stated to me that he was going to Lincoln next week. On Tuesday morning 10 May my attention was called to 15 Paultons Square by Mr Stainsby, I went there about 10.30, Mrs Middleton's daughter let me in and I went into the parlour and saw the bureau open and a number of papers lying on the table and a portfolio. I gathered them up and placed them in the bureau again and I locked it up and put the key in my pocket. I saw the cupboard open where the spirits were kept; I locked that also and put that key in my pocket. I went over the house and searched every part. I did not go into the kitchen, I went upstairs; nothing particular attracted my attention.

'Did you search for a will of Mr Huelin's?' the defence asked, during the cross-examination.

'Certainly not, I have since heard that he made a fresh will and left it unsigned; I saw it with the solicitor – who is now present – when we went over the house together, we searched for papers with the police constables.'

Carter was then asked to concentrate on the events of Saturday, 7 May:

'Mr Huelin told me on the Saturday evening that he had lost his spectacles; he came to my house, I am not clear whether he took tea with me that evening, but he wanted to read the newspaper and said "I have lost my glasses" and I lent him a pair and he read the paper.'

One of the final witnesses to be called by the prosecution was the surgeon, Thomas Ryder. Ryder gave his evidence out of sequence; this may have been because he was unavailable on the first day of the trial or, perhaps, it was the prosecution's ploy to finish with a brutal reminder of the vicious, sickening, and violent facts of the case:

On Wednesday night, 11 May, I was sent for to 15 Paultons Square. I saw the box opened and the deceased woman found in it; she was fully dressed. I examined the body; there was a rope round the neck, it was fastened with a double knot, tight enough to be the cause of death. Blood had issued from the nose and mouth; that arose from the congested condition of the brain, the vessels had burst and blood issued from the nose and the mouth; that was from the stricture round the neck not being removed. There might have been two quarts of blood, perhaps, saturated through the box, trickling over the clothes and on to the floor.

The court heard from two character witnesses called by the defence, Thomas Thynne from Edinburgh and Samuel William Hulbert, both plasterers who gave evidence of the prisoner's previous good character.

Mr Poland then rose from his seat; the court and the public gallery drew breath as they prepared to hear the summing up of the evidence by the prosecution counsel. Mr Poland stood with the confidence of a man who believed his job was done. He informed the court that due to the overwhelming evidence delivered with such succinct clarity by the prosecution witnesses, he did not consider it necessary to exercise his right to sum up the evidence for the prosecution. This stance would be extremely rare in a modern-day criminal trial in England; the prosecution counsel would be very keen to deliver a well-constructed summing-up to a jury. This is the last chance to influence a jury's thinking and ultimately, the verdict, by focusing their attention on the important pieces of evidence which they – the prosecution – believe proves the case. But the legal position in 1870 must be considered: the defendant had no right of speech in a court trial. So it was seen as totally unnecessary in this case to repeat such evidence still so fresh in the minds of the jury.

However, this was the only real opportunity for the defence to argue the defendant's case and as expected Mr Collins stood up; he looked at the jury, making eye contact with each in turn, and straightened his gown. A man's life depended on how he performed over the next half hour or so; this was his opportunity to take the facts of the case and deliver them to the jury in a way that would create doubt in their minds about the guilt of his client. The summing up of the defence case is not recorded in court records, so what follows is a summary from other contemporary records.

Mr Collins started his speech to the jury by reminding them of the solemn duty they were called upon to perform and that it depended upon their verdict whether the prisoner's life should be ignominiously taken away or not. This was Collins' best form of attack, placing the responsibility of this man's life on their shoulders; these were ordinary people, people who were respected within their communities: traders, craftsmen, family men. He would attempt to build up a picture of a very different man portrayed by the prosecution. Could this man, married with two children, really carry out such violent and meaningless destruction of human life?

He stated firstly that there was an absence of motive on behalf of his client to commit the crimes; the deceased treated him well and provided him with a good income. Therefore, he could have no motive for committing such a barbaric act, and even less motive for taking the life of Ann Boss half a mile away.

Collins then turned his attention to the facts of the case. The defence relied on convincing the jury that Walter Millar and the mysterious Frenchman were not one and the same person. Why would a man commit such a dreadful, brutal murder and then employ an acquaintance to dig the hole in which the poor old gentleman was to be buried? Could a man having committed these murders return home to his wife and family, and laugh and joke with them, presenting quite his ordinary appearance? Collins made the point that when returning home there appeared to be no visible traces of blood on his clothes and asked the jury whether if, as suggested, he had only just before destroyed the deceased in the brutal manner described, it was possible for no blood to be seen either upon his clothes or his person?

The defence barrister then turned his attention to the witness Mrs Harriett Middleton and the reliability of her evidence – which was probably no surprise to anybody who had sat through her testimony. He focused on the statement made by Mrs Middleton at the coroner's inquest that the prisoner was not the man who brought the key of No. 15 Paultons Square on the Monday night. He reminded the jury that it was not until the arrest of the prisoner that any suggestion was made that the prisoner was the man who in fact took the key on that night. He pointed out that the prisoner was unable to give any account of the transaction in court, but what he had represented all along was that he acted under the authority of some other person whom he believed to be a relation of the deceased, and if the jury should think that there really was some other man, a foreigner, concerned in the transaction that it would go a great way towards exculpating the prisoner from the charge. Collins suggested that the man, referred to by both mother and daughter, was in the house with them in Paultons Square for nearly three days, and he asked the jury to carefully consider if it was in the bounds of possibility that Millar, with whom they were well acquainted, could have deceived them for so long without either of them realising who the mysterious Frenchman really was.

Discrediting the identification evidence was always going to be the cornerstone of any defence and having suggested that Mrs Harriett Middleton had got it wrong, he turned his focus onto Miss Rebecca Evans. The former tenant of Elias Huelin had attended the Paultons Square address on the Tuesday night and spoke to a man who introduced himself to her as the cousin of the deceased. Collins argued that her inability to identify his client as the person she saw that night when she was asked to do so following his arrest very much strengthened the defence's argument that it really was some other man and not Millar. Collins stated that his client did not deny that it was him who ordered the carman Piper to go to the house to fetch the box, but that he was acting under the authority and orders of another person. As to the prisoner fleeing from the scene of the murder, following the discovery of the blood under the box, Collins submitted that nothing could be more natural: these were the actions of a man who was shocked to find himself in such a position. He panicked and ran.

Collins finished his submissions with a heartfelt plea to the jury that if any doubt, however slight, existed in their minds about the guilt of the defendant then they should not convict but acquit him.

The Lord Chief Justice proceeded to sum up the case for the jury. His speech was both articulate and persuasive. The words used and the inferences made are extremely important and are recorded here as reported by the *London Daily News* on 15 July 1870:

> There could be no doubt that two foul murders had been committed, and the charge against the prisoner depended entirely on circumstantial evidence, upon a variety of facts which were represented to lead to only one conclusion, which was that the prisoner was the person by whom those crimes had been committed. That the deceased gentleman, Mr Huelin, met his death by murderous violence there could be no doubt, and the question they [the jury] were called upon to decide was whether it was made out that the prisoner was the author of the crime? It appeared that on the very day on which the deceased gentleman had been murdered the prisoner employed the witness Payne to dig a hole in which the dead body was afterwards discovered. Who put it there? The prisoner employed the man to dig the drain; he must have filled it up, he had the key of the premises and no one else had access to them. As to what has been said about the imaginary nephew, I cannot discover any trace of evidence to show that such a person had taken a share in this dreadful transaction.

The Lord Chief Justice then turned his attention to the property found on the prisoner, which had subsequently been identified by Huelin's nephew and his best friend John Carter as belonging to him. One notable item was the large sum of money; he commented that such wealth did not correspond to the prisoner's position in life. His Lordship felt compelled to state, with regard to the supposed nephew, that he was unable to discover any evidence to support the suggestion that any such person existed and also commented that although Mrs Middleton might, in the first instance, have entertained some doubt upon the point, it was clear that she was afterwards quite satisfied that the man who was in the house in Paultons Square was the same man who brought her the key, and that man was clearly the prisoner, because he was taken into custody on the spot and the point thus raised by the learned counsel for the prisoner appeared to him to be deserving of little weight.

The Lord Chief Justice's final address to the jury pointed out that:

> Although it is undoubtedly a very fearful thing to send a man of the age of the prisoner to an ignominious death upon the scaffold, still, if the evidence satisfied them that he had been guilty of the awful crime imputed to him, the duty they owed to their country would leave them with no alternative but to say so by the verdict.

The members of the jury retired to discuss their verdict.

13

GUILTY OR INNOCENT?
YOU DECIDE

I t would be quite easy to cut to the verdict. Did Walter Millar convince the jury that a mistake had taken place, or was he convicted and executed at the gallows? Could he have been telling the truth? He admitted, through his barrister, that he was involved with the logistics of arranging and moving a box and other items for a third party, maybe a member of Elias Huelin's extended Channel Islands family or even Edward Huelin himself. Even if this was true, he would still be an accessory to the person who carried out the actual killings. Are we looking too deeply into this? Is the evidence both compelling and convincing and, in your mind, is there any doubt that he *was* a guilty man?

A man's life is at stake – what would you have decided if you had been a member of that jury in July 1870? You have read the evidence, your only disadvantage being that you cannot observe any articulation by the witnesses – but would you have found him guilty, a decision that you knew would send him to the gallows? Let us put ourselves in the position of the jury; this of course will have to be hypothetical as there are no records of their discussions behind closed doors, and neither should there be. So let us look at the evidence the jury would have considered.

As with any group of people brought together, there will be different characters: the vociferous, the shy, the compliant and the obnoxious. Although this group would have been together for only two days (a very short period of time for a murder trial in modern times but quite normal in nineteenth-century England), a natural leader would have surfaced and been elected the jury foreman. The legal system in England demands that a jury come to a unanimous decision: all twelve members must support the same verdict. There is a fallback should this, after a considerable period of time, fail to mate-rialise, and that is the majority decision where the judge will accept a ten-to-two or eleven-to-one decision either way. This outcome is never encouraged by the judge or indeed the legal representatives; the court will give the jury as much time as they need to reach a unanimous decision.

Individual members of the jury would have picked up on specific pieces of evidence throughout the trial to which they, personally, would have added more significance over and above other facts, which in turn would have influenced their leaning toward guilt or innocence. Each member of the jury would have put differing credence on facts presented to them; these points would then be up for discussion and resolution.

The timeline of events would have been important when considering the facts; was it physically possible for Walter Millar to have carried out the crimes alleged against him on 9 May 1870, taking into account the topography of the area and the sightings of him and of the victims? It can be extremely difficult for any witness to remember exactly what time they were in a particular place or witnessed a particular event, especially when asked to recall the event days, weeks or even months after the incident.

Elias Huelin was last seen alive by witnesses in Wellington Square between 11 a.m. and 11.15 a.m., depending on which witness you refer to. One of the witnesses, Thomas Walker, observed Huelin ascending the steps of No. 24 Wellington Square and this was the last sighting of Elias Huelin alive. It should be said that there is no evidence that Walter Millar was in the house when Elias Huelin entered it, or equally, of Millar leaving the address shortly after.

Ann Boss must have been killed between 10 a.m. and 1 p.m. We can accurately base this on the last sighting of her alive by the square-keeper John Hunt at 9 a.m., cleaning the outside step of No. 15 Paultons Square. Hunt then saw Elias Huelin leave the address about 10 a.m., so one can assume that she was alive at this time, and return to the square some fifteen to twenty minutes later, walking past his home to the King's Road end of the square and out of sight. Sidney Ball, the baker, attempted to deliver some bread to the address between 12 p.m. and 1 p.m.; he rang the doorbell and knocked several times but received no answer.

However, it is possible to narrow the time down even more specifically. About 12.30 p.m. Walter Millar met Edward Payne at the Admiral Keppel public house and offered Payne some work digging a drain for him that afternoon. So both murders, if Millar acted alone, must have been committed in a narrow window of time between 11.15 a.m. and 12 noon. Very little was made of the timings of specific events by the defence or indeed the judge; did the jury consider if it was logistically possible for Walter Millar to carry out these horrific murders, conceal the bodies and meet Edward Payne on Brompton Road within one and a quarter hours? We know the distances involved because Inspector Pay from Scotland Yard's detective branch was one step ahead. Realising that distance and timing were going to be paramount in this case, he helpfully and very accurately measured the distances between the critical locations.

The first critical timing is from Wellington Square to Paultons Square which Inspector Pay, for some reason, didn't measure in distance or time. We know that it is approximately a half a mile between the two. A man walking at a good stride without bringing attention to himself would cover about four miles per hour so would take seven to eight minutes to cover this distance. This would mean that if Millar murdered Elias Huelin as he arrived at No. 24 Wellington Square, at 11.15 a.m. at the latest, and spent ten minutes concealing the body, he could leave the house by 11.30 a.m. and be at Paultons Square by 11.40 a.m.; there he could murder Ann Boss, conceal her body within the property or immediately in the box in which she was eventually found. The distance measured by Inspector Pay between Wellington Square and the Admiral Keppel public house was 1,151 yards and would take eleven minutes to walk. If labourer Edward Payne's timing was correct, Millar could have left the Paultons Square address as late as 12 noon (before the arrival of Sidney Ball) and comfortably make the rendezvous with the labourer at 12.30 p.m.; or of course he could still have been in the property, covering up his crime, when Ball called up to 12.15 p.m.

Another issue of timing arises on the night of Monday 9 May: was it possible for Walter Millar to walk from his own house in Seymour Place, having been seen in his kitchen by William Arthur about 12.15 a.m., to arrive, in disguise, at the

house of Mrs Middleton in Sydney Mews between 12.30 and
1 a.m., and hand over the key to Mrs Middleton for 15 Paultons
Square? Logically, yes; the distance between Seymour Place
and Sydney Mews was about half a mile and the most direct
route would be to walk along Brompton Road, which would
take the average man about seven to eight minutes.

Edward Payne walked to No. 24 Wellington Square in
company with Millar on 9 May, where he dug the hole as
instructed by the defendant. Let us consider the evidence of
both detectives Clough and Watts and Dr Thomas Turner
while inside No. 24 on 12 and 13 May. All three observed
what appeared to be smeared blood on the back kitchen floor.
Further blood was found in a cupboard under the stairs, consistent with a person being bundled into this space in a sitting
position. Blood-soaked rags or paper was found in the backyard itself. Importantly Payne, who was at the house probably
only a few hours after the murder of Huelin, five days earlier
than the police and the doctor, did not observe any such blood
stains or blood-soaked materials while he was there. Millar
left the house with Payne on completion of the excavation and
returned home by about 3.30 p.m. He changed and left the
house stating he was going to Hornsey to price up a future job.
It was probably between this time and returning home later
that night when he was seen by William Arthur, shaven and
looking 'guyish', that he returned to No. 24 Wellington Square,
tied a rope around the deceased's neck and dragged him across
the floor of the kitchen leaving a trail of blood, placed him
into the backyard grave, cut off the excess rope, leaving only
11in tied tightly around the victim's neck, and filled the hole
from the spoil nearby, being careful not to disturb the flagstones. He clumsily attempted to clear up the residue of blood
on the kitchen floor, emanating from the wounds inflicted and

the victim's blood-soaked clothing. The judge pointed out to the jury that when Payne left the address the hole was open; when the police first searched the property the hole was filled in and the only persons with a key to the premises during that period of time were the victim Elias Huelin and Walter Millar.

Defence barrister Mr Collins emphasised how it was impossible for a man who had committed such violent crimes not to have any markings of blood on him. But, as we know from the very thorough Inspector Pay, blood *was* found on a pair of trousers in the defendant's room when the house was searched, following his wife's identification of Millar at Chelsea police station.

Another question that may have been posed by the jury was the fact that there were pails belonging to the defendant present in the home of Elias Huelin. Had Millar removed the pails from Wellington Square on 9 May following the murder of Elias Huelin, in order to hide the fact that he had been present at the address earlier in the day, taken them to Paultons Square and left them there by mistake when he had murdered Ann Boss? As we have discussed, he was under severe time constraints. Surely turning up at Mrs Middleton's house as himself with his face wrapped up in a scarf on the morning of 10 May for the keys to Paultons Square, in order to retrieve the pails, could not have been in his original plan. Mrs Middleton stated that she was about to leave for the address, so it would have looked suspicious to have taken the keys and gone ahead, which meant he then had to go to the house with his face still wrapped up, in order to hide the fact from Mrs Middleton that he no longer had his whiskers, just a moustache and a tuft of hair on his chin, so important to his deception. He told Mrs Middleton that morning that Huelin and Boss had gone to the country, something he knew not to be true. He also told Mrs Middleton that he intended to go home for breakfast before meeting her at Paultons Square; this would indicate that he had not gone home that night and probably stayed at the Paultons Square address.

The continuity of the identification evidence was crucial in this case. Although, as pointed out by the Lord Chief Justice, the evidence was all circumstantial, if such evidence is in abundance it can lead to a solid conclusion. William Arthur's evidence supported the change in appearance of Walter Millar to match the description of the man purporting to be Elias Huelin's nephew. Mrs Middleton, although not totally reliable (witnesses are, through no fault of their own, frequently confused about the sequence of events), provided evidence of the Frenchman at her house handing over the key to Paultons Square, a man she saw several times over the next couple of days at the deceased's house.

The following chain of events maintains an unbroken continuity of evidence. Henry Piper entered the house in Paultons Square, discovered the blood emanating from a sealed box and then followed the Frenchman out of the house and into the somewhat hesitant arms of the law, never taking his eyes from him. The chase ensued and the suspect was captured by Piper after remaining in plain view all the while. The prisoner was handed into the custody of PC Coles and escorted to Chelsea police station where he was detained and found to be in possession of a key to the lock which secured the box in which the body of Ann Boss was discovered. The prisoner in custody was then identified as Walter Millar, the plasterer and former employee of Elias Huelin, by his wife.

If you had been sitting in that jury room and considered the evidence available to you, would you have convicted Walter Millar and condemned him to scaffold? Is the evidence so damning that there would have been no doubt in your mind that Millar carried out these despicable crimes? Or do you have the slightest doubt that he may be innocent?

There were still some big gaps in the prosecution's case. The jury must have considered the murder weapon – why was one never found? What about a motive? As so eloquently put by Mr Collins, why did a man with a family, a home in which to live and employment want to bite off the hand that fed him? In a trial full of circumstantial evidence, did the lack of a murder weapon or a proven motive matter?

14

IS MOTIVE
ESSENTIAL?

To establish a motive at an early stage in the case of murder is of great assistance to the detectives investigating. Many lines of enquiry for the investigation team will develop from establishing a motive. Was the crime committed for financial gain, was there any sexual motive, did the victim know their attacker, could it have been a member of the victim's family or was it work-related, a disgruntled employee for example? There are many reasons a person will commit murder; establishing a motive can be crucial to detecting an offender. But is the identification of a motive essential in order to convict a defendant at a criminal trial? The answer is no. Of course if there is a clear-cut motive, the prosecution will use it to assist proving the offence.

In the trial of Walter Millar the motive behind the murders never featured in the evidence. The question was never raised by the prosecution. It is understandable that the prosecution were reticent to mention the lack of a *proven* motive as this may have had a negative impact on their case. So was there ever a motive substantiated in the case of Walter Millar?

The obvious one was material and financial gain; he had been found in possession of items belonging to Elias Huelin. He was wearing clothes that belonged to the deceased; he had money in his pocket as well as deeds to property owned by him. But was he showing signs of extravagant spending during the days before his arrest? He was certainly drinking a lot but most of the alcohol was coming from Huelin's wine cellar. He also bought Elizabeth Green a full set of new clothes. During one of the appearances of the defendant at Westminster Police Court the magistrate, Mr Selfe, asked Inspector Pitt Tarlton what motive had been assigned, if any. Inspector Tarlton replied, 'None, but the love of money, the prisoner had £8 on him when taken and had frequently spoken avariciously of the money the deceased man and woman had.' Was this observation as to motive an opinion formed throughout Tarlton's dealings with the prisoner on the night of his arrest or drawn from his experience as a police officer for a number of years?

James Smith was a painter and glazier who lived in Camera Square off Chelsea's King's Road and had worked with Walter Millar in the past and knew him well. He came forward to police a little time after it had become public knowledge that Millar had been accused and charged with the double murder. Smith, at some time in the recent past, had worked for Elias Huelin in several of his properties. Smith recalled to the police that on one occasion Elias Huelin paid him for his work in the presence of Walter Millar. Millar then commented to Smith, out of the earshot of their employer, that 'he wished he had the old bastard in a room, he would do for him and then go to America'. Smith stated that Millar had made similar comments when the housekeeper Ann Boss had paid them with a gold sovereign each. This evidence was presented at the coroner's court but deemed to be unreliable due to the fact that Smith blamed Walter Millar for taking a lot of work away from him and his statement could have been in retaliation for this. Smith was never called to give this significant insight into a possible motive by the prosecution at Millar's trial.

So was there a motive? Of course there was: somebody in the position of the defendant, who had a young family, a job and a roof over his head, doesn't just kill for the sake of it; the murders were obviously thought out, planned, premeditated. We can surmise what the motive was, but the reasons for these violent killings remained inside the head of Walter Millar.

15

The Murder Weapon

We have all seen on our television screens police dredging rivers and searching waste bins and drains in order to find a murder weapon. We have already discussed both the lack of a proven motive and of hard evidence, somebody witnessing the murders, even a sighting of Millar entering or leaving either of the murder scenes, or being seen travelling on foot or otherwise between one murder scene and the other; we also lack a murder weapon.

Dr Thomas Aubrey Turner, who carried out the post-mortem on Elias Huelin, suggested to the coroner and at the Old Bailey trial that the victim's injuries were consistent with being struck by an implement such as a slater's hammer. A few days later, on 17 May, a letter was received at Scotland Yard from a man who supplied his initials and an address in Camberwell, South London (National Archives MEPO 3/97). He suggests that the weapon used was consistent with a slater's hammer, a tool widely used by roofers in the London area. He even drew a sketch drawing of the slater's

tool showing a cutting edge and a spike emanating from the
blunt side with a simple supporting text that read:

> Sir,
> The above is a drawing of a tool used by slaters – might it not have
> been used by the murderer?

A police memo (National Archives MEPO 3/97) from one of
the investigating team states that such an implement had not
been discovered in amongst the defendant's tools. Of course,
it would be highly unlikely that a murderer would keep the
weapon with which he had destroyed a life. Certainly in 1870
when forensic science was unheard of, tracing the murder
weapon would not have been such a high priority for the
investigating team. Millar never revealed any information to
the police and any further thoughts would be pure supposition.

16

DID HE
ACT ALONE?

W alter Millar's defence case was quite weak, as he had no corroborative evidence to rebut the strong case presented by the prosecution and no evidence to corroborate his own claims of the involvement of a third party. However, the evidence against him was strong and compelling, and had stood up well against cross-examination. The Lord Chief Justice had commented during his summing up that he had not seen a single piece of evidence to support the defendant's claim that he was acting under the authority and orders of another. We have established that physically and logistically he could have committed both murders. But did he have an accomplice, or was this claim merely fiction, concocted by a desperate man who was facing execution for committing two terrible crimes?

Inspector Prescott from Scotland Yard's detective branch was the officer who was sent to Lincolnshire to ascertain if Elias Huelin had indeed travelled to the farm in Navenby. On confirming Huelin had not arrived, he broke the news to Edward Huelin that Ann Boss had been found murdered and it was likely that his uncle had met the same fate. But did Inspector Prescott treat Edward Huelin as a possible suspect in the murder of Boss and the disappearance, at the time, of his uncle? Inspector Prescott was an experienced murder squad investigator and would, without doubt, have gathered evidence of an alibi for Edward Huelin's movements at the time of the murders. The 16-year-old nephew had been tutored in his uncle's business with a view to taking over and eventually inheriting the business; his future was very bright. Would he have had any motive to conspire with Walter Millar to murder his uncle? At such a young age, would he have had the ability to formulate and execute such a conspiracy and the nerve and callousness to kill two people he obviously cared for in cold blood for mere profit?

Was Elizabeth Green somehow involved with assisting Walter Millar? Her story, that she was so drunk she didn't see or remember anything that happened in the basement that night, you may feel was an easy way out, but it has some ring of truth to it, borne out by the fact she was later arrested for being drunk in a public place. Much of her story is corroborated by Police Sergeant Humphrys who had initially arrested her on suspicion of being complicit in the murders. Mrs Harriett Middleton confirms that Green seemed to have been in an inebriated state on her arrival on the Wednesday night. Apart from the fact that she was present at the house when the body of Ann Boss was discovered, there is no evidence to link her with the murders.

The names of two possible associates may shock you: Mrs Harriett Middleton and her daughter. During the inquest into the death of Elias Huelin, the coroner Dr Diplock heard evidence from Inspector Prescott that a jeweller called

W.S. Vincent, who owned a shop on the King's Road, had brought to the police's attention a mystery surrounding a common, worthless ring. It is alleged by Mr Vincent that Mrs Middleton had taken the ring to him to make it smaller. Inspector Prescott told the coroner that because the ring could not be attributed to either of the deceased it did not amount to any material evidence. The coroner, quite rightly, was not satisfied with the explanation and called the witness to give evidence. Vincent introduced himself as the watchmaker and jeweller of No. 336 King's Road. He stated to the coroner that Mrs Middleton had attended his shop on Wednesday, 11 May during business hours, with a small ring that she wished to have reduced in size. She was told by the jeweller that it was not worth doing, but she stated that she wanted it particularly. She was told it would be done in an hour. Miss Harriett, the daughter, came into the shop later that day, before the ring was ready, and gave No. 14 Paultons Square as a forwarding address. The ring was never collected. After a couple of days Mr Vincent took the ring to Paultons Square (the address of Mr Stainsby) and gave a description of the Middletons to a rather confused-looking occupant, who told Vincent they must be referring to the old woman and her daughter next door (No. 15), who were wanted by the police, and that he had better detain them if they came to his shop again. As they never returned, Vincent gave the ring to the police.

Mrs and Miss Middleton were recalled to the inquest and denied ever having been to Mr Vincent's shop and ever having possession of the ring. The two women were positively identified by Vincent as being those of whom he had earlier spoken. The coroner did not see how the ring affected the case before them, unless the ring could be proved to have been in the possession of Mr Huelin or Ann Boss. Sadly, the police seemed to think in the same way, this incident never became part of the prosecution case and, even more surprisingly, never part of the defence, probably because they were never advised of the existence of such contentious evidence (today, this sort of evidence would have to be revealed to the defence under disclosure laws). Is it possible the Middletons had been involved in the murders of Huelin and Boss? The more likely scenario is that they stole the ring during their time at the unoccupied house, took it to Mr Vincent on Wednesday, 11 May and did not return to collect it the next day because of the discovery of Ann Boss's body that night. Mr Vincent's identification of the Middletons was very strong, and coupled with the false address given by the daughter of the house, next to the house in which they were now employed, was too much of a coincidence not to be true. If this evidence was introduced at the trial, especially by the defence, the very least it would have achieved was to discredit both the Middletons' evidence.

17

NINETEENTH-CENTURY POLICING VS TWENTY-FIRST-CENTURY FORENSICS

The use of forensic science as an aid to crime detection was, in 1870, still some years away; the Metropolitan Police's first fingerprint and photographic bureau was not established until July 1901. Edmond Locard (1877–1966), a French scientist and medical examiner, came up with his principle during the First World War that when there is 'contact between two items there will be an exchange. It is impossible for a criminal to act, especially considering the intensity of the crime, without leaving a trace of his presence'. Locard's principle is still taught today in forensic science courses all over the world.

The introduction of DNA evidence did not arrive into the field of crime investigation until the mid-1980s and was very much in its infancy. Of course today DNA evidence is a vital and reliable investigative tool for the police to prove or disprove the involvement of a suspect in a crime, and new advances are being made every year. The police now have the capacity to call on all sorts of experts in many diverse fields:

forensic pathology, entomology, toxicology, odontology, fire-arms and fire investigation and, of course, fingerprints. Every major city in Great Britain is now covered by sophisticated CCTV coverage and this will often record suspects going to, carrying out or escaping from a scene of crime.

Police investigators of 1870 had no such aids to detection; science could not tell them if the blood found on Walter Millar's clothes belonged to one of the murder victims. Science could not identify the transference of fibres between victims and suspect. Fingerprint evidence would probably not have been of any great advantage to the police, as Walter Millar, prior to the offences being committed, had legitimate access to both crime scenes, during which he would have left fingerprints. The Victorians had little idea about crime scene preservation and investigation; the practical science simply did not exist.

In 1870, Superintendent Fisher and his team of detectives had to rely on good, honest police work. The only method open to them was the gathering of evidence through wit-ness interviews and logical thinking, before presenting that evidence to a court of law in a manner that would prove the case against the defendant. Fisher and his team of detectives did this with tenacity, dedication and great professionalism. This was not a particularly difficult case in which to detect and arrest a suspect, but with the lack of real evidence it was a complicated case to prove. The Victorian detectives would have benefitted greatly from the advances in technology enjoyed by modern-day investigators; with the aid of CCTV and forensic science their circumstantial evidence would have been turned into hard irrefutable fact and proved either Walter Millar's guilt or his innocence. A police and Crown Prosecution Service that today relies so much on technology

and forensic science, and often overlooks the importance of
the human witness and their ability to give evidence from a
different perspective, could learn a great deal about the art of
policing from their predecessors of 140 years ago.

18

THE
VERDICT

T he jury filed back into the Old Bailey courtroom late on the second day of the trial, having deliberated for less than thirty minutes. It is often said that if a returning jury looks at the defendant as they take their places, they will probably acquit. If they return and make no eye contact, then the defendant is condemned. Mr Avery, the clerk of the court, asked the jury if they had reached a verdict upon which they all agreed. The foreman of the jury replied:

'Yes, we have.'

'What is the verdict?'

'Guilty.'

Walter Millar must have sat in the dock listening to his fate, and in his prison cell for days afterwards, wondering why he had made so many mistakes, mistakes that would cost him his life. Employing Edward Payne to dig that drain for him, giving the key of No. 15 Paultons Square to Mrs Middleton and failing to remove the box containing the body of Ann Boss himself. If he had personally carried out all of these tasks, could he have got away with the murder of Elias Huelin and Ann Boss? Would the body of Elias Huelin ever have been found? How much time would he have bought himself if he had acted differently? Even Huelin's close associates John Carter and Samuel Stainsby, although suspicious, had accepted that their friend had gone to Lincolnshire. What was the reason for such a complicated plot? He had literally got away with murder as the victims would not have been missed, possibly for weeks, allowing him time to arrange safe passage to America, if that were his intention. Ultimately, an elaborate disguise and a small dog were his downfall.

The clerk of the court asked the prisoner whether he had anything to say as to why sentence should not be passed upon him. Millar looked around the court in silence and made no reply. The Lord Chief Justice placed the black cap upon his head (which in fact was a piece of black cloth which sat on top of the judge's wig) and then addressed Walter Millar, as reported in the *London Daily News*, 15 July 1870:

> You have been found guilty upon the most clear and conclusive evidence of the crime of wilful murder, and it was impossible after the evidence that had been adduced to doubt that you had not only been guilty of the murder of which you were accused in the present indictment but that you had also committed a second murder. There could be no doubt that you have in the most cool and deliberate manner planned the murder of this old gentleman, and that the crime was committed for the sordid and miserable object of obtaining possession of his property. You resorted to a most deliberate scheme and had recourse to the most subtle expedients to conceal your heinous crimes; you must have gone with hands reeking with the blood of one victim to destroy the life of the other. Having destroyed the old man you would not spare the life of the poor woman. You then appeared to

have gone, exulting in your wickedness to your own home and in the presence of your wife and child given way to jests and laughter after committing a crime at which any man possessed of the least feeling must have shuddered.

His Lordship went on to say: 'I cannot find words to express my horror at the conduct of the prisoner and wish he could awaken his guilty soul to something like a sense of the enormity of his crimes and to remorse and penitence.'

His Lordship exhorted Millar to turn his mind to these considerations, and to consider that his doom was fixed and not allow any idle hope or expectation to have any effect. His days were certainly numbered and his Lordship entreated him to devote the short period that remained to him in this world endeavouring to obtain pardon from the only quarter from which a man in his position could receive it. The Lord Chief Justice then sentenced him 'to be taken from this court to a place of execution and be hung by the neck until dead'.

Walter Millar stood in the dock of the Central Criminal Court, showing no reaction or emotion to the fate handed to him. He merely turned to one of the turnkeys and asked, 'When is it to be?' and returned to the cells from whence he came.

When Millar had left the court, the Lord Chief Justice remained seated and directed that Henry Piper stand forward in front of him. His Lordship addressed the man whose sense of public duty and justice had brought many demands for recognition. He told Piper that it was mainly owing to his courage and determination that a man guilty of two of the most atrocious crimes that had ever been committed within his knowledge had been brought to justice, and that he should exercise the power vested in him by Parliament in such a case by ordering him to be paid £50. Those that remained in the court to hear the announcement of the reward showed their agreement with a round of applause. The trial was over and Walter Millar now knew his fate; the execution date was set for 1 August 1870 at Newgate Prison. But this was to be no ordinary execution; the events that surrounded this particular hanging would be notorious and would ensure it was spoken of for many years to come.

19

THE
EXECUTION

T he execution by hanging of Walter Millar, aged 31, took place within the walls of Newgate Prison at 9 a.m. on Monday, 1 August 1870. A huge crowd had gathered outside the prison walls, frustrated and angry that the execution was not to be carried out in public view. Public executions had only been discontinued two years earlier, following the Capital Punishment Amendment Act 1868 which required all executions to be held out of public view.

The executioner was William Calcraft (1800–79), the most famous English hangman of the nineteenth century. Calcraft, born in Baddow, near Chelmsford in Essex, started his working life as a cobbler and during his forty-five-year career is estimated to have executed 450 people. The young Calcraft, who had also worked as a nightwatchman in a brewery in Clerkenwell, had obviously hit bad times and was supplementing his income by selling pies in the vicinity of Newgate Prison (probably during the public executions, which were almost treated like a Bank Holiday) when he met by chance the City of London's hangman John Foxton (1769–1829), who had executed 250 people during his forty-year career, most notoriously the five convicted Cato Street Conspirators, who in 1820, inspired by the antics of the French during their revolution three decades earlier, conspired to kill British Prime Minister Lord Liverpool. They were the last people to be hanged and then beheaded in England, the decapitated heads displayed as a warning to any others with similar intentions.

Foxton recruited the young Calcraft to flog juvenile offenders, for which he received payment of 10s a week. Following Foxton's death in 1829 Calcraft was appointed the official executioner for the City of London and Middlesex at the age of 29. William Calcraft's methods were deemed controversial as he used the short-drop method of hanging, in which the condemned died of strangulation, rather than the long drop which resulted in a broken neck when the trapdoor of the gallows opened. He would place a white cap or hood over the condemned person's head to prevent them from seeing the lever being pulled and attempting to escape the drop. This would also hide from family and friends the agony that they would suffer as a result of his incompetence. Countless victims of his barbaric methods took many minutes to submit to a slow and tortuous death. If the suffering was too prolonged, Calcraft would pull on their legs or even climb onto their shoulders in an attempt to break the victim's neck. It must be remembered that a great majority of William Calcraft's executions were held in front of a baying, screaming crowd, sometimes 30,000 strong, who wanted to see the condemned die in as much pain as possible. Calcraft was seen as a great entertainer, pleasing the horde with his antics.

His most incompetent execution was that of William Bousfield, who had been convicted of murdering his wife and several children in Drury Lane, Covent Garden.

On 31 March 1856, prior to the execution, Calcraft had
received a threat that he would, himself, be killed on the scaffold platform. This unnerved him; he released the bolt on the
trapdoor, saw Bousfield swinging from the rope, turned and
left the scaffold in haste. Bousfield managed to place a leg
back on to the platform, releasing some of the pressure around
his neck. Calcraft's assistant tried to push the condemned
man back off the platform, but was having great difficulty,
as the crowd was going wild with indignation. They wanted
the man to die a horrible death to reflect his terrible crimes,
not to cheat it. Calcraft was called back onto the platform by
the officiating chaplain; he grabbed Bousfield's legs and pulled
him down until he died. The execution of Walter Millar was
about to recreate Calcraft's worst nightmare.

Since Millar had been convicted and sentenced to death he
had proclaimed his innocence to anybody who would listen,
continually blaming a third party – whom he could not identify – for the deaths of Elias Huelin and Ann Boss. There is
evidence that Walter Millar was, to some degree, a religious man,
listening on some occasions to the appeals to pray offered by
the resident chaplain of Newgate Gaol, Rev. F. Jones. However,
there is no doubt that Millar was suffering great mental stress
up to the date of his execution; when the chaplain asked him if
he wished to pray with him, Millar replied that he might if he
liked, but it was indifferent to him whether he did so or not.

On the morning of his execution Millar was offered breakfast, which he declined. Reverend Jones suggested to him that
breakfast might be a good idea in order to better prepare him
for the morning's events. Millar angrily rebuked him: 'No,
I told you so before – I don't want any.'

His conduct up to the execution day had been disturbing,
as the *London Daily News* reported on 2 August 1870:

His conduct has been described by those about him as being most callous and unfeeling; and he never appears to have exhibited anything
like remorse for his dreadful crimes. It appears that the wife of the
wretched man was delivered of a child on Wednesday last, and, at the
request of the prisoner, the child was taken to see him on Friday, but
he did not exhibit any emotion at the sight of his offspring who had
been brought to him under such painful circumstances.

Since Walter Millar's arrest he had been under constant observation due to an apparent intention to kill himself. The time
had come to prepare the prisoner for his execution; present
in the cell were Sheriff Paterson and Undersheriffs Crosley
and Baylis. Just as the process of pinioning him – a feature
of Calcraft executions – was about to begin, Millar escaped
from the hold of the prison warders who were restraining
him and ran head-first into the cell wall. He was prevented
from doing himself any further damage before falling into
apparent unconsciousness. The prison doctor, who was quickly
on the scene, concluded that the prisoner was feigning his
condition. Millar, whether unconscious or not, was placed on
and pinioned to a wooden chair and carried to the gallows.
Calcraft had set the drop at 2½ft, and Millar, who appeared
not to regain consciousness, was executed still seated. As the
trapdoor sprang open, the condemned man dropped the short
distance, chair and all. There were some convulsive movements
for three to four minutes.

William Calcraft, at this point, must have been haunted by
the incompetent hanging of William Bousfield many years
earlier, as Millar appeared to gain a foothold back on to the
platform as he fought for his life. His foot was pushed back
and he eventually died a lingering and horrible death. There
would have been little pity for Walter Millar's plight from

those present, including Henry Piper, who had requested and been granted the right to witness the final moments of a man who to this day will be remembered as one of Chelsea's most notorious killers.

Following the execution, and an additional amount of time in which Walter Millar was left hanging to ensure his death, a black flag was hoisted from the roof of Newgate Prison. This was greeted with a huge roar from the thousands of people who had gathered outside.

Death certificate of Walter Millar with the cause of death given as 'Hanging'.

20

LIFE
GOES ON

The England and Wales National Probate Calendar for 1870 records that on 7 July of that year the personal effects of Ann Boss, valued at under £450, were granted to Charlotte Boss of Fairford in Gloucestershire, her next of kin. An estate of £450 would indicate that a lifetime of servitude to Rev. Elias Huelin had been financially beneficial to her and if she had lived, she would have had a comfortable retirement.

The same records show that on 1 July 1870 the will of Elias Huelin was proved by the oaths of the executors of the will: Rev. John Wilson of Durham House, Chelsea, and Richard Wright (Huelin's solicitor) of No. 57 Lincoln's Inn Fields. The effects were recorded as under £6,000, a handsome sum in those days.

The last will and testament of Elias Huelin raised an anomaly which resulted in issue being raised in the court of the vice chancellor, as reported in the *London Illustrated News* on 26 November 1870:

A suit is in progress in the court of Vice-Chancellor Malins for the administration of the estate of the Reverend Elias Huelin, one of the victims of the Chelsea tragedy. Elias Huelin had left a legacy to Ann Boss his servant, the other victim of the crime and a question was raised [probably by Edward Huelin who had, it would seem by bringing this court action, formed a penchant for money] obviously as to which of the two were murdered first. In the case of the servant dying before the testator her legacy would have lapsed. While in the other event it would fall to her legal representatives. The matter at present stands over for enquiries.

The case returned to the vice-chancellor's court in July 1871, again reported by the *London Illustrated News* (29 July 1871):

A suit to administer the estate of the late Elias Huelin who was, together with his housekeeper Ann Boss, murdered at Brompton in May 1870 by Walter Millar, came before Vice-Chancellor Malins last Saturday. As Huelin had by his will made a bequest in favour of Ann Boss it became necessary to ascertain which was the survivor. This question was referred to the Vice-Chancellor in chambers and the result was a certificate that Ann Boss was the survivor. The Vice-Chancellor, on Saturday, made an order in accordance with the certificate.

Ann Boss never married, nor did she have children, so her entire estate (including the bequest by Elias Huelin) went to her sister Charlotte Boss and with insufficient personal details about Charlotte, it has not been possible to trace her life after her sister's death. A police report (National Archives MEPO 3/97) following the trial and conviction of Walter Millar confirms that the green wooden box in which Ann Boss was found and the clothes in which she had been murdered had been destroyed by the police.

Edward Huelin, the young nephew of Elias Huelin, would have inherited a large part of his uncle's estate when he came of age. Records have been a little kinder in an effort to follow what must have been a very traumatic period of Edward's life. It is possible that he returned to Jersey following the trial of Walter Millar, as he does not feature in any 1871 mainland census or for that matter records pertaining to the Channel Islands. However, he does appear ten years later in the United Kingdom census of 1881 and is found to be a trainee solicitor lodging in Richmond, Surrey. The 35-year-old Edward married Edith Theodore Eliza Francis on 22 September 1887 in Surbiton, Surrey. By the time of the next census in 1891 the fully qualified solicitor had moved to one of his uncle's former properties – presumably now belonging to him – at No. 14 Paultons Square, Chelsea, formerly rented by Samuel Stainsby and next door to his uncle's house and the scene of Ann Boss' murder. The census shows that he and Edith now had a son, Edward Scotter Huelin, aged 2, and two domestic servants, a cook and a nanny. They have the addition of a daughter called Grace, aged 8 in 1901. The last census currently available (1911) shows Edward, aged 58, and his family having moved to No. 11 Elsham Road, Kensington.

Very little is known of Margaret Ann Millar; she would probably have changed her name and moved from London, maybe back to her family in Scotland. It seems her late husband left her and their children with little security.

Henry Piper married Sarah Ann Piper in 1862, and they had five children: four daughters and one son. Piper is recorded on the 1871 census still residing with his family at No. 112 Marlborough Road, Brompton, as a self-employed greengrocer. Sadly, he died six years later, in 1877, aged 42. He left his wife, the sole executor of his estate, goods under £1,500. Let us hope he had time to enjoy his £50 award.

Mrs Harriett Middleton and her husband William are recorded on the 1871 census as living at a new address,

No. 17 Thurloe Place, South Kensington. William died the following year. Harriett was still alive in 1881 and living with her daughter Harriett, her husband and five children. Harriett senior died in 1886, aged 76.

On the 1871 census Samuel Stainsby, his wife Elizabeth and their nine children had moved to Sutherland Gardens, Paddington. By 1891 he had a new wife, Fanny, and they were living with three of Stainsby's children in Heanor, in Stainsby's native Derbyshire. By 1901 he had returned to West London with three of his youngest children but Fanny is absent from the record. Samuel Stainsby died in 1909, aged 81.

Lieutenant Colonel Sir Edmund Henderson was appointed Metropolitan Police Commissioner in 1869 following a distinguished military career. He became extremely popular with his men, abolishing petty regulations introduced by the former commissioner, including allowing his subordinates to grow facial hair and the freedom to vote for a political party. He was also opposed to the cut in police pensions and wages which led to the first police strike in 1872. He was responsible for the 'fixed point system' (officers had to be at a certain point on their beat at a certain time) and he increased the size of the force's detective branch to over 200 detectives. He resigned from his post in February 1886 following his perceived inaction at the Trafalgar Square riot, which followed protests against economic hardship by London's poor.

Superintendent William Fisher moved on from 'T' division in October 1888 to 'A' division, which covered the Westminster area of central London. He remained here until 1892 when he retired on a full pension following twenty-five years' service.

Inspector Pitt Tarlton was from a policing family. Pitt served just another year following the Walter Millar case, retiring on medical grounds following an assault in July 1870 in which he received a serious head wound. The reason recorded for his retirement, at the age of 44, on police records was that he was simply 'worn out'. Tarlton then found employment as a foreman with the Gas Light and Coke Company at its Imperial gasworks in Sands End, Fulham – the same works that provided temporary work for Frederick Vince, a prosecution witness. Tarlton appears in the 1881 census aged 54 and living on King's Road with his wife Caroline, aged 47 years, daughters Mary and Frances, and a young son, Edward, aged 4. Pitt Tarlton died in Fulham at the age of 67 in 1897, and his wife died two years later.

James Pay, who joined the force in 1851, was promoted to sergeant at Wandsworth in 1858 and wore the collar number 8P. He was then further promoted to inspector on 16 March 1867 and was transferred to 'A' division where he became one of the most experienced detective inspectors at Scotland Yard. Sadly, he died from heart disease in September 1875 while in his prime, aged just 43.

Detective Edward Clough, one of the two officers who discovered the corpse of Elias Huelin, was of small stature – only 5ft 9ins. He was born in Woolwich and joined the police in 1863 at the age of 21 having previously been trained as a brass turner. Following this investigation he progressed to the rank of detective sergeant in 1880 and retired on a full police pension in 1889.

Police Sergeant John Large lived locally for the remainder of his police career, retiring at the rank of inspector in April 1879. He was a family man who appeared to have four children, three daughters and one son.

Public executioner William Calcraft reluctantly retired in 1874 aged 74, after forty-five years in post. Calcraft received a pension of 25s a week from his former employer, the City of London. He died at his home in Poole Street, Hoxton, in London's East End on 13 December 1879.

AFTERWORD

Of course, the death of any person in such violent, premeditated circumstances is as much a concern for us today as it was in 1870. As ever, this was not an anomaly and there will be many more horrific crimes to follow; we witness the depressing realism of our violent society every day in the media. But, victims aside, the people who suffer most are those left behind. Walter Millar's wife and children would have been deeply affected by these atrocious crimes, as would the family and friends of Elias Huelin and Ann Boss.

The number of homicides recorded by police (source: Office of National Statistics) in 2012–13 is 552 with a 90 per cent detection rate; this includes domestic and parental murder. Homicide, including murder, is at its lowest level since 1983; a reflection of the reduction in violent crime, which is down by 8 per cent. Murder in today's society is, thankfully, extremely rare, and most people in Great Britain will never experience the loss of a loved one through violent acts such as those that have been disclosed in this book. But when it happens, it changes lives forever.

BIBLIOGRAPHY

Bland, James, *The Common Hangman: English and Scottish Hangmen before the Abolition of Public Executions* (Wiltshire: Zeon Books, 2001)
National Archives, Kew – MEPO 3/97
'Proceedings of the Old Bailey 1674 to 1913', www.oldbaileyonline.org

Newspapers
Daily Telegraph, 14 May 1870
Illustrated Police News, 21 and 28 May 1870
London Daily News, 12, 17 and 21 May 1870
London Daily News, 14 and 15 July 1870
London Daily News, 2 August 1870
London Illustrated News, 26 November 1870
London Illustrated News, 29 July 1871
The Morning Advertiser, 14 May 1870
The Star, 17 May 1870
The Times, 13, 14, 16, 19 and 21 May 1870
The Times, 13, 14 and 15 July 1870
The Times, 2 August 1870

INDEX

Lightning Source UK Ltd.
Milton Keynes UK
UKOW04f1048190914

238830UK00001B/1/P